EXPLORE THE WORLD

Social Studies Projects and Activities

o-w-w-w-w
w-a-a-a-a-a

by Denise Bieniek. M.S.
Illustrated by Ellen Sasaki

Troll
CREATIVE
TEACHER
IDEAS

Troll Creative Teacher Ideas was designed to help today's dedicated, time-pressured teacher. Created by teachers for teachers, this innovative series provides a wealth of classroom ideas to help reinforce important concepts and stimulate your students' creative thinking skills.

Each book in the series focuses on a different curriculum theme to give you the flexibility to teach any given skill at any time of the year. The wide range of ideas and activities included in each book are certain to help you create an atmosphere where students are continually eager to learn new concepts and develop important skills.

We hope this comprehensive series will provide you with everything you need to foster a fun and challenging learning environment for your students. **Troll Creative Teacher Ideas** is a resource you'll turn to again and again!

Titles in this series:

Metric Conversion Chart		
1 inch = 2.54 cm	1 foot = .305 m	1 yard = .914 m
1 mile = 1.61 km	1 fluid ounce = 29.573 ml	1 cup = .24 l
1 pint = .473 l	1 teaspoon = 4.93 ml	1 tablespoon = 14.78 ml

Contents

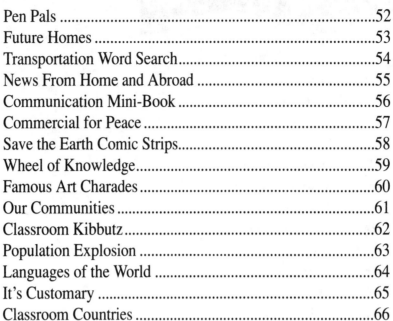

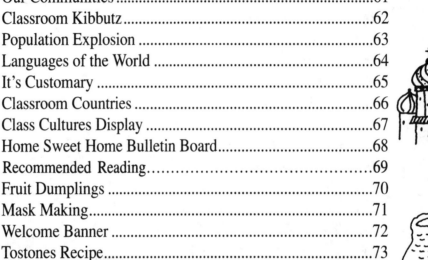

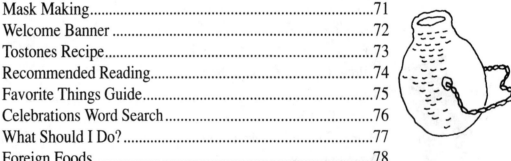

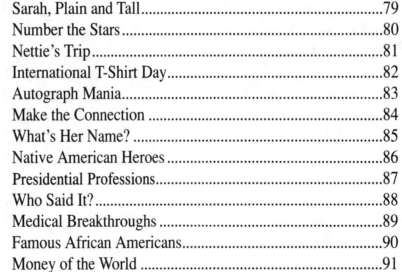

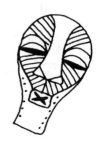

School Days Interviews

Brainstorm with students about what school may have been like for their grandparents and great-grandparents. Write students' comments on the chalkboard.

Have the class come up with topics for a short questionnaire to hand out to older relatives, friends, and neighbors. Some suggested topics:

country of origin
place where person spent his or her childhood
school name
curriculum
typical day at school
after-school activities
lunch
class size
classmates
name of a favorite teacher and why he or she
   was liked

Encourage the children to administer the questionnaire to as many people as possible. Have students write down each person's responses on a separate piece of loose-leaf paper. If desired, students may tape their interviews, but they should still write summaries of the questionnaires to share with the class.

Compare and contrast the ideas from the brainstorming session with the actual experiences of the interviewees. Compare and contrast education today with education past. Ask students to name some things they see as advantageous and some things they see as disadvantageous in today's educational system.

Reproduce the art on page 6 once for each student to make a cover for his or her interviews. Punch three holes along the left side of the cover. Then tie the pages of the questionnaire together with the cover on top. Place the interview books in the reading center or social studies center for students to read during free time.

school in Kenya

ugali for lunch

playing Kigogo

5

SCHOOL DAYS
INTERVIEW

Compiled by:

_____

Age ____

Time Line Folders

MATERIALS:

old magazines
scissors
9" x 12" oaktag
glue
markers
folder with pockets

DIRECTIONS:

1. Look through old magazines for any 9" x 12" picture and cut it out.
2. Glue the picture to a 9" x 12" piece of oaktag.
3. On the blank side of the oaktag, make a time line featuring a period in history that the class has been studying. Write the events of the time line from top to bottom instead of left to right. Draw a line between events. Do not add the dates to all the events, only the first and last.
4. Cut apart the time line on the lines between events.
5. Store the game in a folder that has pockets. Reproduce and cut out the directions below to tell students how to put the time line together.

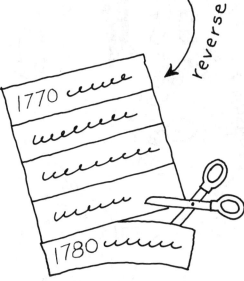

> 1. Read the events on each rectangle. Put them in order from top to bottom on the right side of the open folder, from the event that happened first to the event that happened last.
>
> 2. To check that the order of events is correct, close the folder. Then turn the folder over to the back and open it. If the picture is put together correctly, then the time line is in order!

6. Create several time line folders and encourage students to make their own time lines. Place on a bookshelf or loan them to other classes.

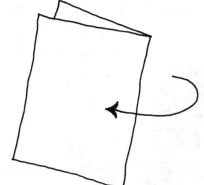

Family Mobile

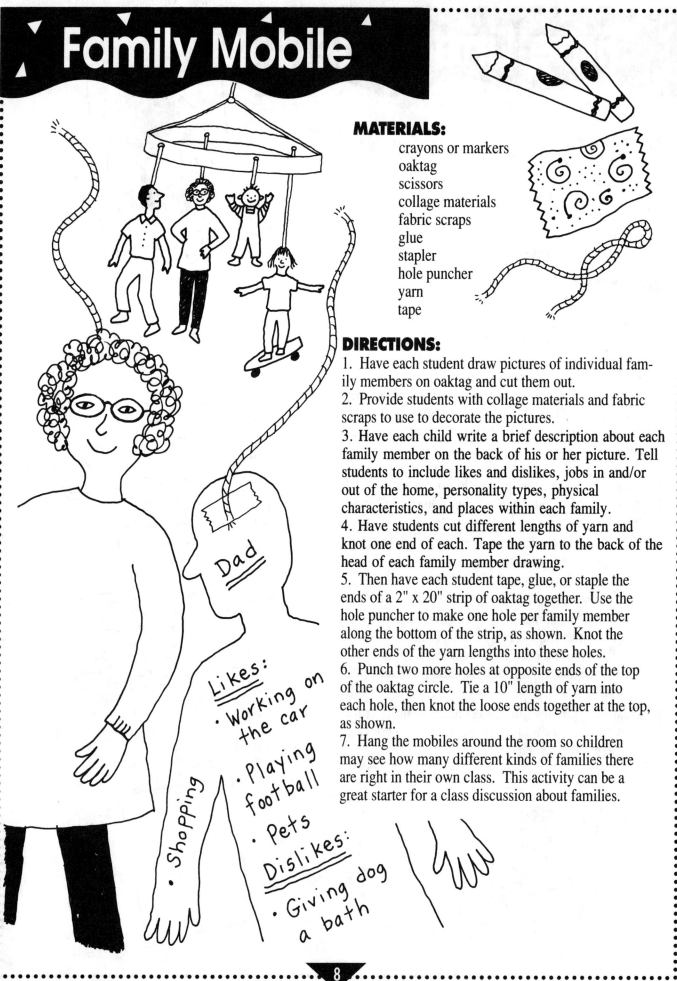

MATERIALS:

crayons or markers
oaktag
scissors
collage materials
fabric scraps
glue
stapler
hole puncher
yarn
tape

DIRECTIONS:

1. Have each student draw pictures of individual family members on oaktag and cut them out.
2. Provide students with collage materials and fabric scraps to use to decorate the pictures.
3. Have each child write a brief description about each family member on the back of his or her picture. Tell students to include likes and dislikes, jobs in and/or out of the home, personality types, physical characteristics, and places within each family.
4. Have students cut different lengths of yarn and knot one end of each. Tape the yarn to the back of the head of each family member drawing.
5. Then have each student tape, glue, or staple the ends of a 2" x 20" strip of oaktag together. Use the hole puncher to make one hole per family member along the bottom of the strip, as shown. Knot the other ends of the yarn lengths into these holes.
6. Punch two more holes at opposite ends of the top of the oaktag circle. Tie a 10" length of yarn into each hole, then knot the loose ends together at the top, as shown.
7. Hang the mobiles around the room so children may see how many different kinds of families there are right in their own class. This activity can be a great starter for a class discussion about families.

Dad

Likes:
• Working on the car
• Playing football
• Pets
• Shopping

Dislikes:
• Giving dog a bath

Seven Wonders

Name _____

The Seven Wonders of the Ancient World were ancient art and architectural works that were famous for their awesome splendor. Only one of the Seven Wonders—the Egyptian Pyramids at Giza—still exists today.

Write a brief description for each of the Seven Wonders of the Ancient World, telling what made it unique. Then, on a separate piece of paper, name seven modern-day wonders.

1. Hanging Gardens of Babylon _____

_____

2. Temple of Artemis at Ephesus _____

_____

3. Egyptian Pyramids at Giza _____

_____

4. Colossus of Rhodes _____

_____

5. Lighthouse of Alexandria _____

_____

6. Statue of Zeus at Olympia _____

_____

7. Mausoleum at Halicarnassus _____

_____

Canadian Time Travel

Name _____

You've just invented a time machine that can take you back to any period in Canadian history! Draw lines to match the events below to their correct dates. Then choose one of the years to travel to in your time machine, and tell about your adventures on a separate piece of paper.

1. British and Canadian troops fight off two major invasion attempts by the United States.   1898

2. Marquette and Jolliet sail down the Mississippi River.   1642

3. Canada holds a world's fair in Montreal.   1867

4. New Brunswick is established as a colony.   1673

5. The British North America Act established the Dominion of Canada.   1784

6. Samuel de Champlain of France founds the city of Quebec.   1812-1815

7. The Yukon becomes a Canadian territory.   1967

8. Canada joins the League of Nations.   1774

9. French missionaries found the city of Montreal.   1920

10. The Quebec Act is passed, giving French Canadians political and religious rights.   1608

Native American Tribes

Name _____

Write the names of the locations where each of the following Native American groups lived during the 1700's.

1. Cherokee

2. Iroquois _____

3. Pueblo _____

4. Navajo _____

5. Cree _____

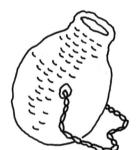

6. Seminole _____

7. Pawnee _____

8. Eskimo _____

9. Nez Percé _____

10. Sioux _____

On a separate piece of paper, write about one of these Native American tribal nations. Describe the area where they lived, what things they did, and what made this nation different from other tribal nations. Finally, tell what has become of this Native American group, and where they now live.

Name That State

Name _____

Many words and names of places in the English language are derived from Native American words. Look at the names of the states in the column on the left. Match each state to its Native American origin in the column on the right.

1. Utah

2. Connecticut

3. Kansas

4. Nebraska

5. Texas

6. Illinois

7. Michigan

8. Hawaii

9. Idaho

10. Tennessee

A. In Shoshone, *ida* means "salmon" and *ho* means "eaters."

B. From the Caddo word *teysha*, which means, "Hello, friend!"

C. In Chippewa, *majiigan* means "clearing."

D. The Apache word *Yuttahih* means "one that is higher up."

E. The word *Kawayi* means "homeland" for this tribal nation.

F. From the Mohican word *KwEnhtEkot*, which means "long river place."

G. The Cherokee word *tanasi* means "unknown."

H. Derived from the Iroquois word for "plain."

I. From the word *Illni*, meaning "man or warrior."

J. From the Omaha word for "broad water," which refers to the Platte River.

Revolution Elocution

To help introduce a study unit about the Revolutionary War, divide the class into groups of five to six students each. Assign a particular event in the war for each group to dramatize. Some suggestions are:

Boston Tea Party
Paul Revere's ride
Boston Massacre
Signing of the Declaration of Independence
George Washington crossing the Delaware River
Cornwallis surrenders at Yorktown
Battle of Lexington and Concord
Triumph of John Paul Jones

Help the groups write short scripts for their dramatizations. Encourage students to create costumes, props, and scenery for their skits. (If necessary, let students work with more than one group.)

When the groups have rehearsed a sufficient amount of time, let them perform their skits for the rest of the class. After all the skits have been seen, have the class work together to write a narrative that ties the skits together in chronological order. Then let the class perform the entire play for parents, friends, and other classes. You may also wish to attach the written skits and narratives together in order and leave the entire play in the reading center for all to enjoy.

Letters Home

During a study unit about the Civil War, divide the class into two groups. Tell one group that they will pretend to be part of the Confederate army, and tell the other group that they will be part of the Union army.

Ask the children in each group to research what life was like for the soldiers and other people in their army. If possible, help students find original sources, such as diaries, letters, or other personal accounts from people involved in the war. Discuss the hardships that soldiers on both sides had to face (i.e., hunger, illness, injury, etc.), and why each side was willing to endure such hardships in order to win the war.

After students have completed their research, ask each child to write a letter "home" to his or her family from the battlegrounds of the Civil War. Students may wish to be army captains, privates, or young boys who have just joined the war; or, they may wish to be army doctors or nurses, cooks, spies, or other people who helped the Confederate or Union cause.

Let students read their letters to the other members of their groups. Then have each group choose several letters to share with the rest of the class. Attach the letters collage-style to a bulletin board entitled, "Civil War Letters."

Transportation Time Line

Name _____

Using the dates from the box below, fill in the year that each method of transportation was first invented or used.

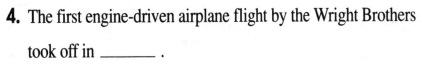

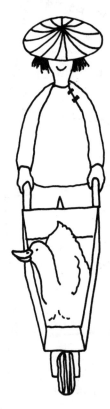

1. The steam locomotive was first used in _____ .

2. The wheelbarrow was invented in China in _____ .

3. The first workable steamboat was invented in the United States in _____ .

4. The first engine-driven airplane flight by the Wright Brothers took off in _____ .

5. In _____ , cable cars were invented.

6. A human-powered submarine was invented in _____ .

7. The gasoline-powered automobile was invented in Germany in _____ .

8. The Sumerians are credited with inventing the wheel in _____ .

9. The self-propelled bicycle was invented in Scotland in _____ .

10. The first hot-air balloon was launched in _____ .

| 3500 B.C. | 1885 | 1787 | 1903 | 1783 |
| 1620 | 44 A.D. | 1873 | 1839 | 1804 |

What do you think transportation will look like in the future? On a separate piece of paper, draw a picture of a 21st-century method of transportation and explain how it works.

20th Century Toss-Up

Name _____

This history teacher has mixed up all his note cards! Now he's not sure which events occurred in the 20th century, and which occurred in other centuries. Draw a line through each event that did not happen in the 20th century.

Columbus sets sail for a new route to India.

The automobile is invented.

The first human being sets foot on the moon.

Thousands of people move to California to cash in on the gold rush.

Magellan circumnavigates the globe.

The state of Israel is founded.

Ellis Island opens the door for immigration to America.

The first atomic weapons are made.

The United Nations is formed.

World War I begins.

The Wright Brothers successfully fly their first plane.

The first television show is broadcast.

Chinese Dynasties

Name _____

Fill in the time line below to show the approximate period of each of the following Chinese dynasties.

Chinese Dynasties

1600 BC 1000 BC 250 BC 0 AD 250 AD 500 AD 750 AD 1000 AD 1300 AD 1500 AD 1900 AD

Great Wall of China

| Shang | Zhou | Qin | Han | Sui |
| Tang | Song | Ming | Qing (Manchu) | Yuan (Mongol) |

On a separate piece of paper, name a significant development that occurred in China during one of the dynasties mentioned above.

Wars of the World

Name _____

Read the descriptions of each battle below. Then write the name of the war or battle on the line provided.

1. The end of Germany's 890-day siege of this city marked Russia's turn toward victory.

   _____

2. This battle was Napoleon's final defeat. _____

3. This American victory convinced France to help the colonies in the war against the British.

   _____

4. One of the most important battles of the Civil War, it is also known for the speech given there by Abraham Lincoln. _____

5. Norman invaders defeated the English in this battle in 1066.

   _____

6. This war ended when some Greek warriors, hidden inside a huge wooden horse, launched a surprise attack on the city of Troy. _____

7. This battle, "a date which will live in infamy," brought the United States into World War II.

   _____

8. The sinking of four Japanese aircraft carriers turned the tide in the Pacific in World War II.

   _____

9. American defenders, including Davy Crockett, held off the Mexican army for 13 days.

   _____

10. Americans led by Andrew Jackson defeated the British in the final battle of the War of 1812.

   _____

On a separate piece of paper, write a report about one of these battles. Include information about the events leading up to the battle, what took place during the battle, and the effects the battle had on the groups involved.

Recommended Reading

Reading historical fiction helps children understand more about different periods of history. Place the appropriate books from the list below in the classroom reading center when studying a particular social studies unit. Encourage students to read the books and share their thoughts with classmates.

Middle Ages
The Whipping Boy by Sid Fleischman (Greenwillow, 1986)
Adam of the Road by Elizabeth J. Gray (Viking, 1942)

Colonial America
Caddie Woodlawn by Carol R. Brink (Macmillan, 1973)
Calico Bush by Rachel Field (Macmillan, 1987)
The Witch of Blackbird Pond by Elizabeth G. Speare (Houghton Mifflin, 1958)
Amos Fortune, Free Man by Elizabeth Yates (Dutton, 1967)

American Revolution
My Brother Sam Is Dead by Christopher Collier and James L. Collier (Macmillan, 1984)
Johnny Tremain by Esther Forbes (Houghton Mifflin, 1943)
Sarah Bishop by Scott O'Dell (Houghton Mifflin, 1980)

Recommended Reading

Civil War
Charley Skedaddle by Patricia Beatty (Morrow, 1987)
Rifles for Watie by Harold Keith (HarperCollins, 1957)

Post-Civil War
Sarah, Plain and Tall by Patricia MacLachlan (HarperCollins, 1985)

1900's
Roll of Thunder, Hear My Cry by Mildred Taylor (Dial, 1976)

World War II
Anne Frank: The Diary of a Young Girl by Anne Frank (Doubleday, 1967)
Number the Stars by Lois Lowry (Dell, 1990)

Tracing Family History

Name _____

Research your family's history to find out what cultural background you have. Here are some hints to help you fill in the charts. Use the chart below as a model to make a family history chart of your own.

- If you are not certain of a date, place the year in parentheses.
- Use women's maiden names (last names given at birth).
- If a person has two different spellings for his or her name, write the second spelling in parentheses.

Begin filling in your chart with the help of a parent or a grandparent. Later, you may wish to use sources available at a local library.

	Parents	Grandparents	Great-Grandparents

Ancestry Chart

Family of: _____

_____
father's father
b. _____
m. _____
d. _____

_____
father's father's father
b. _____
m. _____
d. _____

_____
father's father's mother
b. _____
d. _____

_____
father
b. _____
m. _____
d. _____

_____
father's mother
b. _____
d. _____

_____
father's mother's father
b. _____
m. _____
d. _____

_____
father's mother's mother
b. _____
d. _____

_____
you
b. _____
m. _____
d. _____

_____
sibling
b. _____
m. _____
d. _____

_____
sibling
b. _____
m. _____
d. _____

_____
mother's father
b. _____
m. _____
d. _____

_____
mother's father's father
b. _____
m. _____
d. _____

_____
mother's father's mother
b. _____
d. _____

_____
mother
b. _____
m. _____
d. _____

_____
mother's mother
b. _____
d. _____

_____
mother's mother's father
b. _____
m. _____
d. _____

_____
mother's mother's mother
b. _____
d. _____

b = born
m = married
d = died

Tracing Family History

Reproduce the chart below as many times as necessary for each student.

Family Information Chart	**Chart Number:** _____

Name: _____   Religion: _____

Birth date: _____   place: _____

Marriage date: _____   place: _____

Date of death: _____   place: _____

Date of burial: _____   place: _____

Mother's maiden name: _____   Father's name: _____

Occupation: _____

Residences: _____   date: _____

_____   date: _____

_____   date: _____

_____   date: _____

Spouse's name: _____   Refer to Chart Number: _____

Spouse's father: _____   Refer to Chart Number: _____

Spouse's mother: _____   Refer to Chart Number: _____

Children of this marriage in order of birth (note multiple births):

1. _____   Date: _____

2. _____   Date: _____

3. _____   Date: _____

4. _____   Date: _____

5. _____   Date: _____

6. _____   Date: _____

Misfit

Name

Circle the word that does not belong in each group.

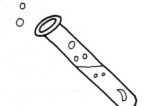

1. serf   noble   Victorian   medieval

2. Bastille   Louis XVI   Revolution   Greenland

3. Mesopotamia   Roman   Ur   Euphrates

4. economy   monarchy   democracy   socialism

5. John Cabot   Thomas Edison   Leif Ericson   Juan Ponce de León

6. Maya   Inuit   Aztec   Inca

7. Nile   Amazon   Sahara   Seine

8. Andes   Pacific   Rockies   Alps

9. Franklin   Lincoln   Kennedy   Roosevelt

10. da Vinci   Michelangelo   van Gogh   Pasteur

Government Crossword Puzzle

Name _____

Find the answers to the clues below and fill in the puzzle.

Across

2. This type of leader holds absolute power and authority.

3. A system based on the ownership of all property by the community as a whole and where one political party dominates, as in the former Soviet Union.

4. The Thirteenth Amendment, which was passed in 1865, outlawed this in the United States.

6. A type of government headed, either absolutely or constitutionally, by a king or queen.

8. The national legislative branch of Great Britain, composed of the House of Commons and the House of Lords.

Down

1. These are the heads of various departments, i.e., the official advisers to a president, king, or governor.

2. A government where the people hold the ruling power directly or through elected representatives.

5. The President of the U.S. who issued the Emancipation Proclamation on January 1, 1863.

7. The legislative branch of U.S. government made up of the Senate and House of Representatives is called _____.

Crazy Contents

Name _____

The table of contents for this history book is all mixed up! Rewrite the list to show where each country really belongs.

Europe	**Europe**
Japan	_____
Brazil	_____
Kenya	_____
North America	**North America**
France	_____
China	_____
Peru	_____
South America	**South America**
Denmark	_____
Thailand	_____
South Africa	_____
Canada	**Asia**
Asia	_____
Israel	_____
Poland	_____
Mexico	_____
Argentina	_____
Africa	**Africa**
India	_____
United States of America	_____

African Latitude and Longitude

Name _____

1. The lowest point in Africa is Lake Assal in Djibouti at 509 feet below sea level. Between what latitudes and longitudes is it located?

_____

_____

2. The highest point in Africa is Mt. Kilimanjaro in Tanzania, which stands 19,340 feet tall. Between what latitudes and longitudes is it located?

_____

_____

3. If you were told to find a lost person at 20 degrees North Latitude and 10 degrees East Longitude, what desert would you be looking in? _____

4. Mount Cameroon is a volcano in Cameroon. It last experienced activity in 1982. Which degree of longitude is it closest to? _____

5. Swahili is a language spoken by about 46 million people in various countries. One of these countries is located at 0 degrees Latitude and 20 degrees East Longitude. Which country is it?

_____

Fiddle, Faddle! Geography Game

Gather the class together and sit in a circle in front of a world map. Choose a leader to stand in the middle of the circle.

Each player will pick the name of a country from the world map; make sure each student chooses a different country (no duplicates).

When the leader says, "Go," all players will begin to repeat the names of their chosen countries. When the leader says, "Fiddle, one, two, three" and points to a player, that player must go to the map and point out the country the player to his or her right was repeating. If the leader says, "Faddle, one, two, three" the player being pointed to must go to the map and point out the country the player to his or her left was repeating.

Players have until a count of three to find the country. If a player is able to find the correct country on the map, he or she gets to be the new leader. If not, the same leader continues the next round.

SPAIN!

GHANA!

CHILE!

PAKISTAN!

LAOS!

Travel Time

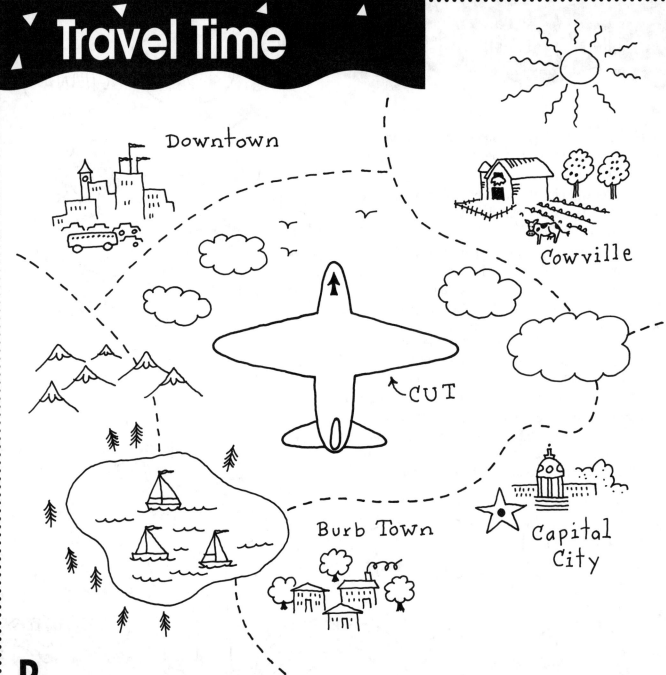

Downtown

Cowville

CUT

Burb Town

Capital City

Reproduce the small airplane on this page once for each student. Distribute, and ask students to write their names on the planes and cut them out.

Attach a piece of tape to each plane.

Tape a map of the country on the chalkboard at eye level. Explain to the class that they will be taking a trip.

Choose one student to go first. Blindfold the player and spin him or her around three times gently. Point the player towards the map. He or she must try to tape the airplane on the map.

When unblindfolded, the player must read the name of the location where the airplane has landed. Then ask

the player to tell anything he or she knows about that part of the country. Encourage other students to help out by sharing information they have about the region.

Continue playing until all the children's airplanes are on the map. Then ask each student to write a short report about the region where his or her plane has landed. Give students suggestions about what to include in their reports, such as:

climate	manufacturing
topography	population
farming	landmarks
history	things to do

Name That State

Name _____

Write each state's abbreviation within its border, or draw an arrow to indicate its location.

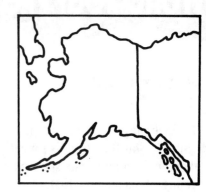

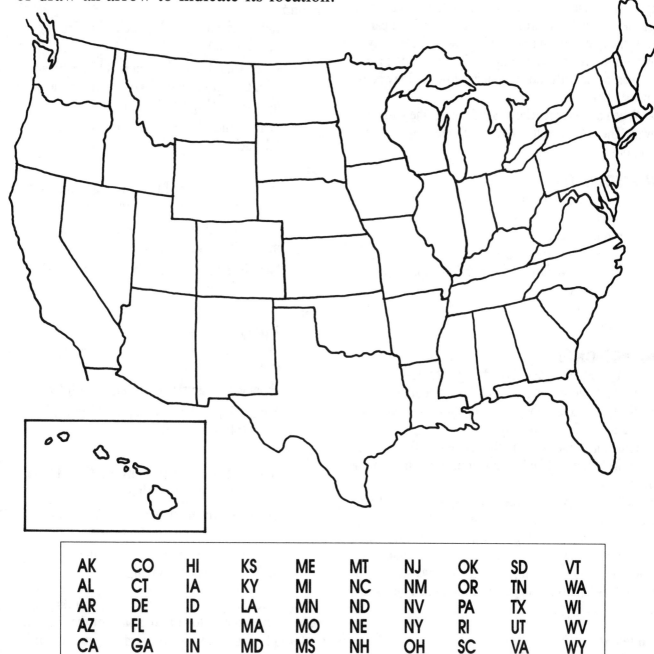

AK	CO	HI	KS	ME	MT	NJ	OK	SD	VT
AL	CT	IA	KY	MI	NC	NM	OR	TN	WA
AR	DE	ID	LA	MN	ND	NV	PA	TX	WI
AZ	FL	IL	MA	MO	NE	NY	RI	UT	WV
CA	GA	IN	MD	MS	NH	OH	SC	VA	WY

World Tour File-Folder Game

HOW TO PLAY:
(for two to four players)

1. Each player places his or her playing piece on "Start." Shuffle the cards for each country and place them in the appropriate spots on the board. The youngest player goes first.
2. The first player rolls the die and proceeds to the appropriate suitcase. The sticker on the suitcase will let the player know from which pile to take a card.
3. If the question on the card is answered correctly, the player receives a bonus coupon. If the question is not answered correctly, no coupon is allowed. Play continues clockwise.
4. When a player reaches "Start" again, the game is over. The winner is the player with the most bonus coupons.

MATERIALS:
> crayons or markers
> scissors
> glue
> letter-size file folder
> different-colored construction paper
> clear contact paper
> envelope
> die

DIRECTIONS:
1. Reproduce the game board on pages 32–33 once. Reproduce the game cards and bonus coupon on page 31 thirty times and the "How to Play" instructions above once. Color and cut out.
2. Glue the game board to the inside of a file folder. Glue the "How to Play" instructions to the front of the file folder.
3. To make playing pieces, cut 1" squares from four different colors of construction paper.
4. On the back of each game card, write a question about one of the countries featured in the game. Countries may be changed by laying new "stickers" on the suitcases. Some suggestions for game questions are:

United States
Mt. Everest is found in the United States. True or false? (false—border of Tibet and Nepal)

The war between the colonies and what country led to the independence of the United States? (England)

How many U.S. states begin with the letter "M"? (eight)

Name five Presidents of the United States. (answers will vary)

Ireland
Ireland is called the Emerald Isle. True or false? (true)

By kissing this stone, you will be endowed with the "gift of gab." What is the name of the stone? (Blarney Stone)

What is the traditional language of Ireland? (Gaelic)

Italy
What is the name of the building found in Italy that actually leans? (Leaning Tower of Pisa)

Is the lira a type of musical instrument or money in Italy? (money)

Paris is the capital of Italy. True or false? (false—Rome)

Japan
Japan is made up of four large islands and thousands of smaller ones. True or false? (true)

What is the capital city of Japan? (Tokyo)

Mount Fuji is the highest peak in Japan. True or false? (true)

Canada
Niagara Falls is shared between Canada and what other country? (United States)

The two official languages of Canada are English and _____? (French)

What group of Europeans were the first to discover Canada? (Vikings)

5. Laminate the game cards, coupons, and playing pieces. Glue an envelope to the back of the file folder to store playing pieces, game cards, coupons, and the die.

World Tour File-Folder Game

World Tour File

Folder Game

Around the World in One Night

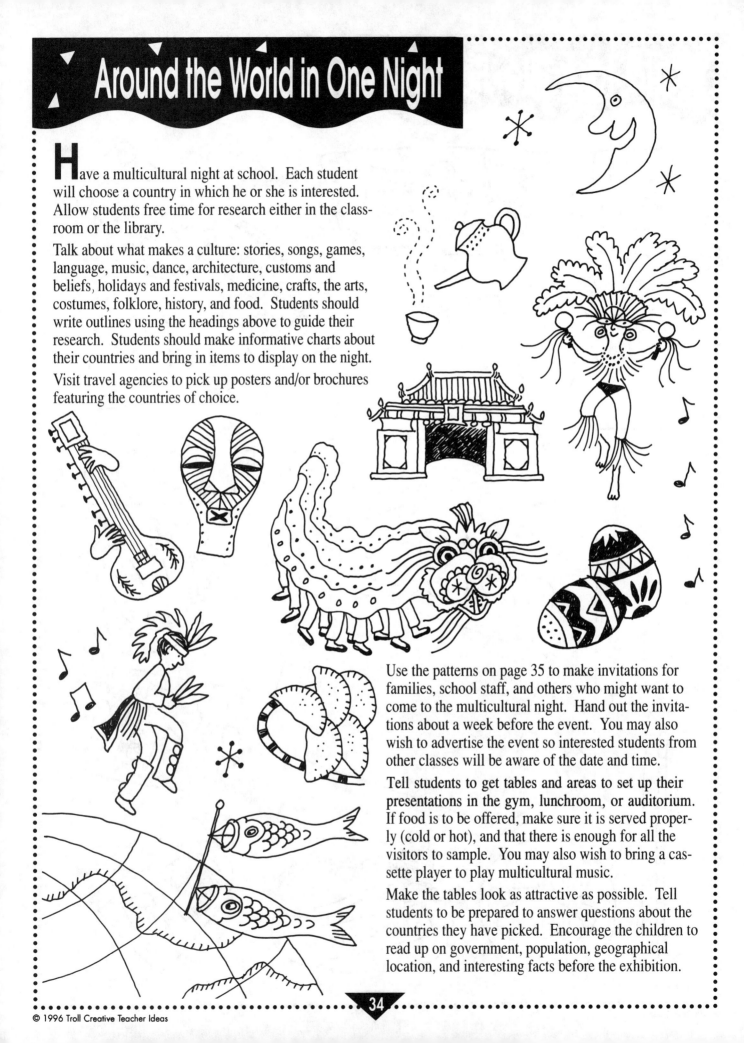

Have a multicultural night at school. Each student will choose a country in which he or she is interested. Allow students free time for research either in the classroom or the library.

Talk about what makes a culture: stories, songs, games, language, music, dance, architecture, customs and beliefs, holidays and festivals, medicine, crafts, the arts, costumes, folklore, history, and food. Students should write outlines using the headings above to guide their research. Students should make informative charts about their countries and bring in items to display on the night.

Visit travel agencies to pick up posters and/or brochures featuring the countries of choice.

Use the patterns on page 35 to make invitations for families, school staff, and others who might want to come to the multicultural night. Hand out the invitations about a week before the event. You may also wish to advertise the event so interested students from other classes will be aware of the date and time.

Tell students to get tables and areas to set up their presentations in the gym, lunchroom, or auditorium. If food is to be offered, make sure it is served properly (cold or hot), and that there is enough for all the visitors to sample. You may also wish to bring a cassette player to play multicultural music.

Make the tables look as attractive as possible. Tell students to be prepared to answer questions about the countries they have picked. Encourage the children to read up on government, population, geographical location, and interesting facts before the exhibition.

Vacation Plans

Name _____

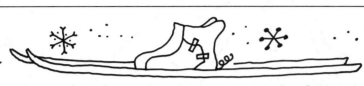

Using information from the chart, answer the following questions.

CITY	Jan. TP/RF	Feb. TP/RF	Mar. TP/RF	Apr. TP/RF	May TP/RF	June TP/RF	July TP/RF	Aug. TP/RF	Sept. TP/RF	Oct. TP/RF	Nov. TP/RF	Dec. TP/RF
Boston	30/4	31/3.7	38/4.1	49/3.9	59/3.5	68/2.9	74/2.7	72/3.7	65/3.4	55/3.4	45/4.2	37/4.9
Helena	18/.7	26/.4	32/.7	42/1.0	52/1.7	60/2.0	68/1.	66/1.2	56/.8	45/.7	31/.5	23/.6
Nome	9/.8	3/.5	7/.6	18/.6	36/.5	45/1.2	51/2.2	50/3.1	42/2.3	28/1.3	16/.9	4/.7
San Juan	77/3	77/2	78/2.3	80/3.6	79/5.6	80/4.7	82/4.9	82/5.9	82/6	81/5.9	80/5.6	78/4.7

TP/RF = Temperature/Rainfall

Where would you take a summer and a winter vacation?

Summer _____

Winter _____

What clothing would you bring with you?

Summer _____

Winter _____

What types of activities could you do while there?

Summer _____

_____

Winter _____

_____

An Explorer's Thoughts

Ask each student to choose a famous explorer from history. Tell students to research and take notes about how the explorer traveled, what discoveries were made, when the voyages took place, what happened along the way, what happened when they arrived at their destinations, who they saw (if there were people), and what the situation was upon the return to the starting point (if there was a return).

After students have completed their research, ask each child to write five journal entries about one or more of the journeys taken by the chosen explorer. Students should write their entries in the first person, as if they are the explorers. Tell students to provide as many details as possible and to use their imaginations. The entries may be as graphic, funny, scary, or detailed as desired. Students should also include a map of their journeys in their journals.

Divide the class into groups and have each student share his or her journal with the other children in the group. The members may ask questions or make comments on the journals they hear. Have one or two members a day speak until all the journals in each group have been heard.

Combine all the journals into one big book and loan it to other classes to read, or keep it on the bookshelf for use during free time.

37

Worldwide Charts

Name _____

Use the information in the charts on page 39 to answer these questions.

Weather Chart

1. If you like milder temperatures in summer, where would you be likely to take your vacation?

_____

2. You should bring along an umbrella if you plan to visit this state. _____

3. It's winter and you would love to spend some time in a warm climate. Where would you go?

_____

4. You're driving through this state in the summer and it's very hot. You're afraid the car will

overheat. What state is this? _____

Summer Olympics

1. Which team has a prime number for the total amount of medals it won? _____

2. One team's total is the same as 4 to the second power. Which team is it? _____

3. If you multiply this team's silver and bronze medals together, the total comes to 42. Which team

is it? _____

4. Which team's gold medal total is a multiple of 5? _____

5. Two-thirds of this team's medal total are bronze. _____

Air Distances

1. These distances have a 7 in the hundreds place. Which are they? _____

_____

2. Put the distances in numerical order from smallest to largest. _____

_____

3. Which distance between cities is closest to half the distance from London to Melbourne?

_____

4. Write the distances that are multiples of 2. _____

_____

Worldwide Charts

Name _____

Weather Chart

| | Normal Temperatures | | | | Normal Annual Precipitation (inches) |
| | January | | July | | |
	Max.	Min.	Max.	Min.	
Alabama	61	41	91	73	56
Hawaii	80	65	87	73	110
Michigan	31	16	83	61	32
Nevada	55	33	105	76	22

Summer Olympics (Barcelona, Spain—7/25/92–8/9/92)

| | Final Medal Standings | | | |
TEAM	Gold	Silver	Bronze	Total
Unified Team	45	38	29	112
Cuba	14	6	11	31
Bulgaria	3	7	6	16
Denmark	1	1	4	6

Air Distances

	Berlin	Melbourne	Rio de Janeiro
Beijing	4,589	5,643	10,768
London	583	10,500	5,750
Montreal	3,740	10,395	5,078
Warsaw	322	9,598	6,455

Fact Sheet

Name _____

Read the facts about each place below. Then use reference books to find out more information. Use the pattern on page 41 to create a Venn diagram based on the facts you've learned.

Hawaii

Hawaii is the 50th (and last) state of the United States. Composed of 132 islands in the North Pacific Ocean, Hawaii is subtropical and maintains mild temperatures year round. Sugar cane and pineapples are Hawaii's most important crops.

There is a unique mixture of cultures on the Hawaiian islands. People from Japan, Korea, the Philippines, Southeast Asia, Tahiti, Tonga, Polynesia, Samoa, the U.S., and European countries have settled there. The state's main industries are tourism, defense, manufacturing and construction, and agriculture.

China

China is a socialist country. About 80% of the people live in rural villages. Because of its tremendous size, there are many temperature zones: subtropical in the far South, sub-arctic regions in the North, a monsoon climate in the East, and an arid climate in the Northwest.

China is also made up of many different cultures. Many people live in cities or on farms. There are also some people called nomads who move from place to place with their herds of goats and sheep. China is a leading producer of sugar cane, cabbage, tea, and wheat.

Lapland

The Lapps are a traditional people who live in an area called Lapland, which is located above the Arctic Circle in the upper reaches of Scandinavia. Most Lapps are nomads, and their lives center around the herds of reindeer they own, which provide them with meat for food, hides for clothing and blankets, and bones for spoons, needles, and other useful things.

Lapps travel by dog sledge. In the spring and summer they live in the mountains, and in the fall and winter they move down to the lower plateaus. Lapp houses resemble teepees and are called *lavo*. Some people also live in huts when they are in the mountains.

Fact Sheet

Name

set 1

set 2

set 3

Are We Almost There?

Answer these questions based on the map below.

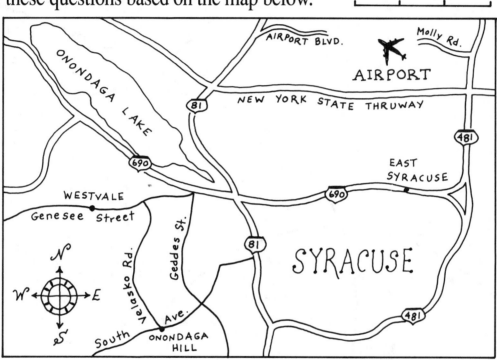

1. What is the best way to get to the airport from Westvale? _____

_____

_____

2. Approximately how many miles long is Onondaga Lake? _____

3. How would you get from the New York State Thruway to Onondaga Hill? _____

_____

_____

4. You have landed at the airport. You need to get to East Syracuse. In which direction will you

travel? _____

5. What are the names of the roadways that intersect at Onondaga Hill? _____

_____

Canadian Crossings

Name _____

Fill in the names of the Canadian rivers, lakes, and bays on the map below.

Hudson Bay	Ottawa River	St. Lawrence River	Baffin Bay
Great Bear Lake	Fraser River	Lake Winnipeg	Albany River
Saskatchewan River	Severn River		

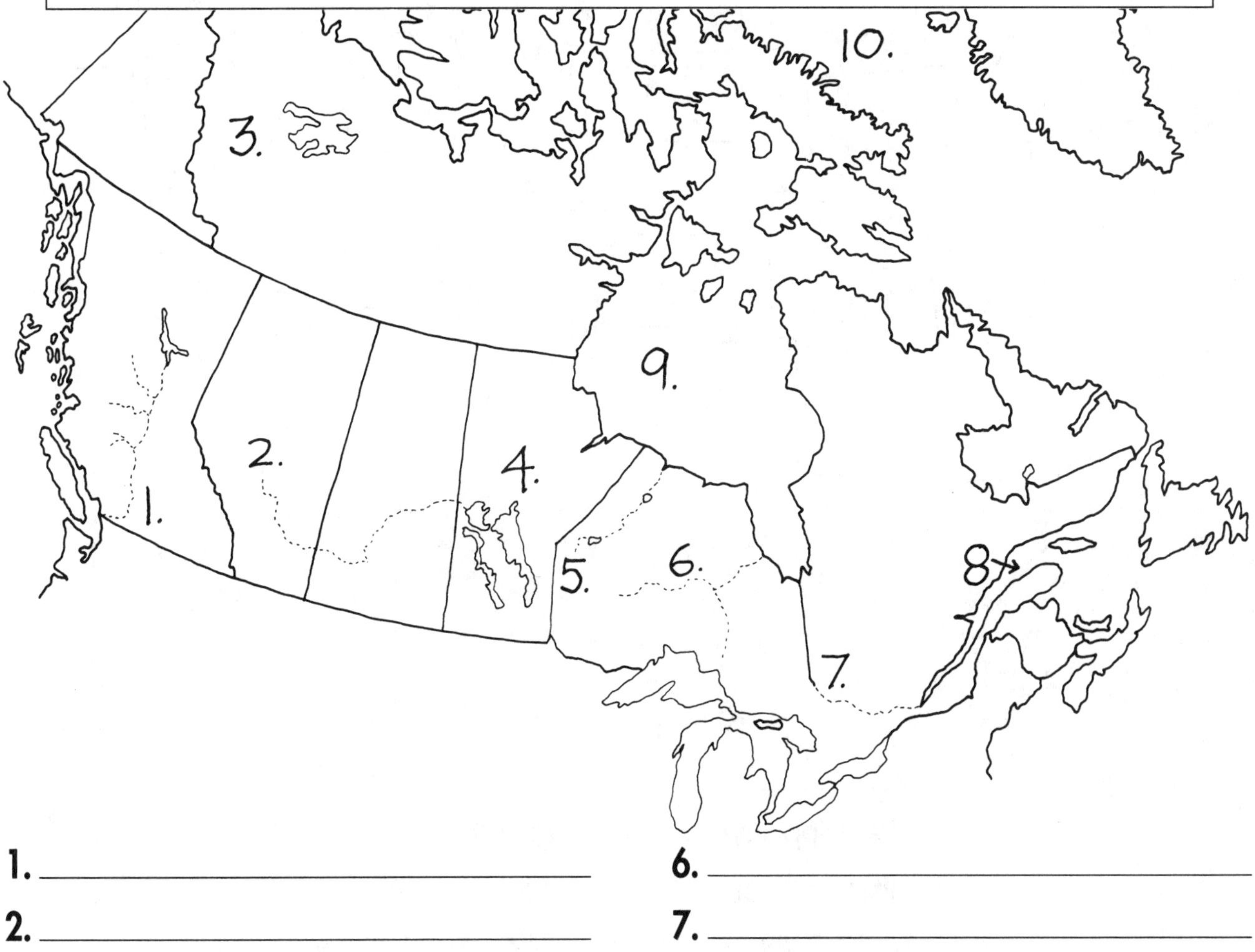

1. _____   6. _____

2. _____   7. _____

3. _____   8. _____

4. _____   9. _____

5. _____   10. _____

A River Runs Through It

Name _____

On a separate piece of paper, write the name of each state where the rivers listed below are found. (Remember—a river may flow through more than one state!)

Mississippi River	Rio Grande
Missouri River	Allegheny River
Snake River	Sacramento River
Hudson River	Arkansas River
Colorado River	Ohio River

Capital Caper

Name _____

Find the hidden names of the capitals of the states listed in the box below. The words may be hidden up, down, forward, backward, or diagonally.

```
P L H G I E L A R T L I T T H
T U S D O R I C A I P M Y L O
L T A L L A H A S S E E J R N
K A C A K E I P N M E V K O O
H U R O L R I O S C C U C H L
D L A Y P V T F Y R N V E J U
N V M S P N A N G K E H R L L
O Y E H E U A U C N D U R U C
M H N R S B L O N N I Y E A H
H B T D L N R T I O V R I P E
C V O A O E B R T H O J P T Y
I I P S L V I E S T R L K S E
R D E T T E E N U L P U Y V N
N C T P I O M R A U A J J M N
E I R A L E N A S H V I L L E
L U L U L O N O H J U N E A U
```

Alaska	Florida	Minnesota	Rhode Island	Washington
Arkansas	Hawaii	New Jersey	Tennessee	Wyoming
California	Illinois	New York	Texas	
Delaware	Massachusetts	North Carolina	Virginia	

Hemisphere Happenings

Name _____

Unscramble the names of the countries listed below. Then write an "N" on the line provided if the country lies in the Northern Hemisphere, and an "S" if it lies in the Southern Hemisphere.

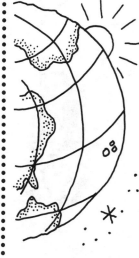

NREANIAGT _____

DAIIN _____

EDSINAZWTLR _____

EWN LAZEDNA _____

DAAANC _____

NICAH _____

REUP _____

BAQOEUMIZM _____

UOSHT REKAO _____

GUYURUA _____

ALDINFN _____

SATAIUALR _____

ALPDON _____

COXIEM _____

YGETP _____

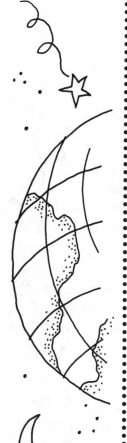

City Search

Name _____

Find the names of the cities listed below in this word search puzzle. Then put the cities in order according to their population. Write a "1" next to the city with the greatest number of inhabitants, a "2" next to the second largest city, and so on.

Tokyo _____
New York _____
London _____
Beijing _____
Paris _____
Buenos Aires _____
Toronto _____
Mexico City _____
Seoul _____
Berlin _____
Madrid _____
Lisbon _____
Vienna _____
Cairo _____
Nairobi _____
Delhi _____
Athens _____
Rio de Janeiro _____
Sydney _____
Moscow _____

```
I S R C A I M O S C O W Q T
B E R L H N I L R E B U P O
E U K L A D O T Q L C A T R
I F E J I S I K U E R E M O
J D E N A I R O B I A J E N
I Y U G O O E I S V G O X T
N S Q J Y S A O R I A C I O
G Y V W G N A R K V X I C M
N D E A N N E I V A E M O A
O N A T H E N S R L G V C D
B E O R I E N A J E D O I R
S Y L S O U Q Y G T S L T I
I V E Y L O N D O N Y E Y D
L T A D N O E O Y K O T V A
```

Our Favorite Cities

MATERIALS:

9" x 12" construction paper   brochures and magazines
glue   crayons or markers
hole puncher   yarn or string

DIRECTIONS:

1. Have a class discussion about major cities around the world. Encourage students to brainstorm names of cities, and tell what makes them important. Write the names of the cities on the chalkboard.

2. After 30-40 cities have been named, let each child review the list. Using reverse alphabetical order, have each student come to the chalkboard and choose one of the cities to use as the focus of a research book. Tell each student to write his or her initials next to the chosen city. (Only one student may choose each city.)

3. Discuss the kinds of things that students may want to include in their books. Some suggested topics are:

history	educational system
manufacturing	transportation
economy	museums and historic sites
food	culture
population	

4. If possible, have students collect magazines, brochures, and other visual and informational materials from travel agencies and embassies about the different countries. Help students outline and organize their books into sections that focus on the various topics they have chosen to cover.

5. When students are satisfied with their outlines, provide them with 9" x 12" construction paper to use for the pages in their books. Students may glue pictures from brochures or magazines or draw pictures on each page, and provide captions and text as well.

6. Have each child create a cover and think of a title for his or her book. Then place the pages and cover together in their proper order and punch three holes along the left side. Tie the pages together with string or yarn.

7. Encourage students to show their books to the rest of the class while giving brief oral reports about the cities. Place the books in the classroom reading or social studies center as reference books for all to use.

Postcard Switch

Name _____

On a separate piece of paper, fill in the names of the countries from which these postcards might have been sent. Choose your answers from the countries listed in the box below.

China	Russia	Peru	France	Italy
Egypt	Brazil	Kenya	Greece	United States

Natural Wonders

Name _____

Break the code to find out the names of these natural wonders!

A = △   G = •   M = ∧   S = ☉   Y = #

B = \\   H = ▽   N = ⊢   T = ▣   Z = ◬

C = ▢   I = /   O = —   U = <

D = ～   J = ▱   P = ⊠   V = ⌐

E = ⌄   K = ⊥   Q = ◇   W = ⌐

F = ●   L = ✓   R = ∧   X = ◈

1. _ _ _ _ _ _ _ _ _ _ _

2. _ _ _ _ _ _ _ _ _ _ _ _

3. _ _ _ _ _ _ _

4. _ _ _ _ _ _ _ _ _ _ _ _

5. _ _ _ _ _ _ _ _ _

6. _ _ _ _ _ _ _ _ _ _

7. _ _ _ _ _ _ _ _ _ _ _

8. _ _ _ _ _ _ _ _ _ _ _ _

Exploration Itineraries

Name _____

Oh, no! The travel agency has given the world explorers below the wrong itineraries. Draw lines to match each explorer's name to the proper voyage.

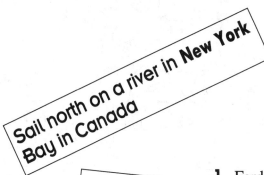

Sail north on a river in **New York**
Bay in Canada

China

Tahiti
New Zealand
Australia
Hawaiian Islands

South Pole

Newfoundland

Rocky Mountains
Pacific coast

West Indies

1. Ferdinand Magellan
2. James Cook
3. Christopher Columbus
4. Meriwether Lewis & William Clark
5. Leif Ericson
6. Vasco Núñez de Balboa
7. Ponce de Léon
8. Roald Amundsen
9. Marco Polo
10. Hernando Cortes
11. Henry Hudson
12. Sir Edmund Hillary and Tenzing Norgay

Mexico

Mount Everest

Florida

Circumnavigate the globe:
Sail west from Spain to Cape Horn
Philippines

Isthmus of Panama
Pacific Ocean

Pen Pals

Here are the names of two organizations that bring students together with other students who are interested in becoming pen pals:

Dear Pen Pal
P.O. Box 4054, Dept. UF
Santa Barbara, CA 93103

Caravan House
132 East 65th St.
New York, NY 10021

Dear Pen Pal is sponsored by the Big Blue Marble television show. Each student must send his or her name, address, age, sex, and interests (in English only) to the address listed above. The organization will match up students with other children from the United States or other countries. This is a free service. **Caravan House** will send you a *Pen Friend's Guide*, which costs $1 (U.S.) per copy. The guide lists pen pals, ages 6 to 20, and adults, in 50 countries.

Once a pen pal has been matched to a student, encourage him or her to think up some good letter starters. Some suggestions:

- Write about yourself—what you look like, your home, neighborhood, and school. Enclose a photograph if possible.
- Sports—what you like to play and watch.
- Write about what you do after school and on weekends.
- Vacation spots you have visited.
- Weather in your area.
- Holidays and celebrations.
- Hobbies and other areas of interest.

Encourage students to share the responses they get from their pen pals with the class. Begin a letter-writing time set aside just for pen pal letters. Display the photographs of the students' pen pals on the board and indicate where they are from.

Future Homes

MATERIALS:

crayons or markers   9" paper plates
oaktag   scissors
white thread   tape
stapler

DIRECTIONS:

1. Ask each child to draw a background of where he or she might like to live in the future on the inside of a paper plate (i.e., undersea, outer space, in the sky, underground).

2. Then ask each student to draw a picture on oaktag of what his or her house will look like. Encourage students to use oaktag to create other objects that might be nearby, such as buildings and other houses, trees, transportation, or people wearing future clothing. Cut all these pictures out.

3. Have students arrange these objects on the background, then tape a short length of thread to the top of the back of each object, as shown.

4. Tape the loose end of the thread to the top of the back of the paper plate. When the plate is held up, the objects should hang suspended in their proper places. (Students may need to adjust or add tape to get the positions right.)

5. Cut the center out of another paper plate and discard it. Staple the outer part of the plate over the first plate, with the back facing front, so it forms a frame for the picture, as shown. Ask students to color or decorate this frame in the theme of the future home.

6. Display the future homes with student essays about what they imagine life will be like in the future.

(back of object)

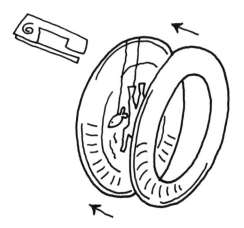

(staple plates, right sides together)

Transportation Word Search

Name _____

Find the names of the different forms of transportation listed below. The words may be written up, down, forward, backward, or diagonally.

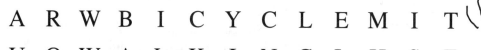

A R W B I C Y C L E M I T

U O W A L K I N G L H S E

T M O N H E L M I E S A G

T R A I N S F E L V H I D

E A P O C T K I D A D L E

K C L U B L C C A T O B L

C H A R I O T G I O C O S

O Q N G P J P C A R T A G

R Z E T H O R I S E C T O

V L E M A C B O H A T R D

R R H E T M O O E S R O H

bicycle	chariot	helicopter	rickshaw
ship	camel	dog sledge	horse
rocket	train	elevator	plane
sailboat	walking	car	

News From Home and Abroad

Ask each student to bring in an article from a newspaper or magazine, or watch the news at night on television and write a paragraph about a story that interests them.

Discuss the stories in a news show format. Have each student come up to a news desk and report his or her piece. Encourage students to share their opinions about what is happening in the world. Ask students to think up solutions to some of the problems that are occurring at home and around the world.

Hold a mock debate when students are more familiar with current events. Assign someone to be the Secretary-General of the United Nations. Have students volunteer to be the diplomats whose countries' problems will be featured for the debate. Some suggestions for debate are:

> human rights
> territorial disputes
> getting involved in wars between other countries
> homelessness
> poverty
> drug abuse
> ecology
> education

Divide the class into groups to help the diplomats prepare for the debate. Use the solutions created by the students during current event discussions. How will one country's actions affect other countries? Try to work out compromises that all parties will find acceptable.

If the students feel their ideas are worthy of notice, start a letter-writing campaign to government officials. Keep track of the responses, and talk about students' reactions to what the officials have to say.

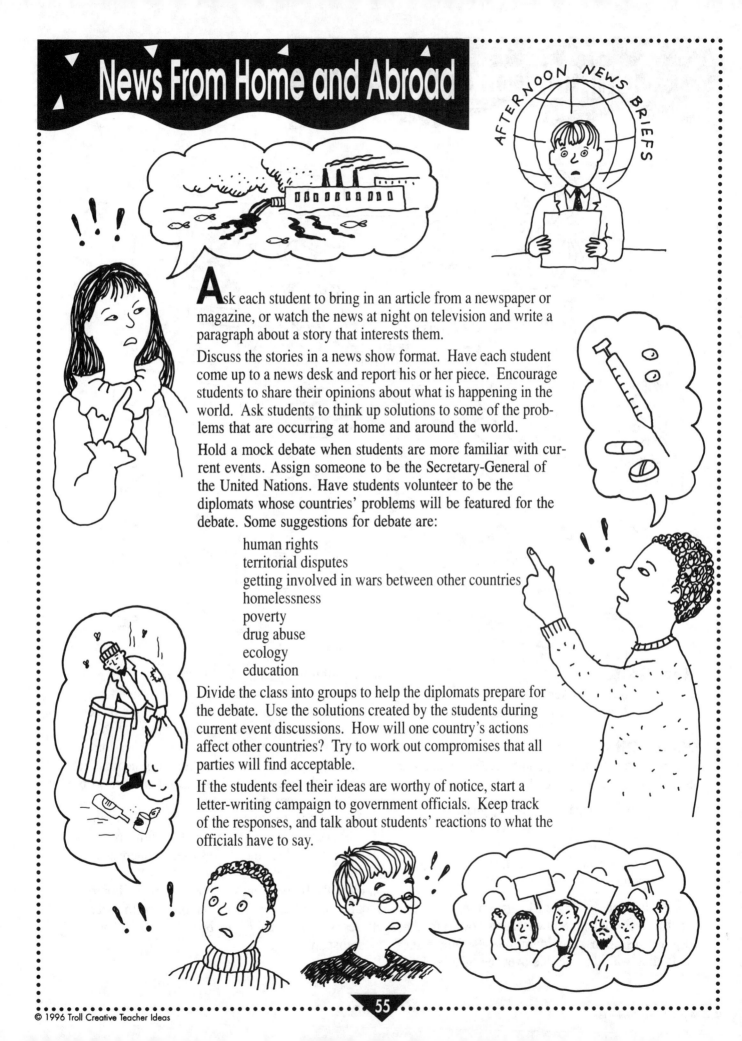

Communication Mini-Book

MATERIALS:

    crayons or markers
    4 1/2" x 24" construction paper strips

DIRECTIONS:

1. Brainstorm about how people have communicated since the beginning of time. Some suggestions:

body language	sign language
grunting	word of mouth
letters and other	computers
documents	satellite
phone	

2. Distribute one 4 1/2" × 24" strip of construction paper to each student. Show students how to fold the strip into 6 sections, accordion style. Be sure to start the folding with the left side over the middle, as shown—this will be the cover of the book.

3. Tell each student to think of a cover design for a book about communication, and write in his or her name as the author. Encourage students to choose forms of communication that show a progression through time. Draw one or two forms of communication for each time period chosen. Add another strip of construction paper if necessary.

4. Ask students to write a short paragraph on each page or every other page about certain forms of communication in which they are especially interested (sign language or computers, for instance).

5. Place the books alongside books from the library about communication. Share the books with other classes, or loan some of the books to the school library for a display.

Commercial for Peace

Gather the class together to talk about peace. Ask a volunteer to begin by saying something about peace and/or hatred. It may be an opinion, a fact, or an experience she or he has had.

Continue discussing until all the children have had a chance to speak. Encourage students to respond or add to comments made by others.

Divide the class into groups of five. Tell students that each group is going to make a "commercial" for children their age that will help promote peace and end hatred. The commercial may be designed for radio, television, or print (i.e., newspaper or magazine).

Suggest to students that the commercials may be dramatized, sung, spoken, or drawn. When each group has completed its commercial, have them perform it for the class.

Let the class discuss the points made in the commercials and what made them good (i.e., young people reaching out to their peers, bright colors to attract attention, popular music young people can relate to, using language familiar to young people).

Share the commercials with other classes, and discuss with them their ideas for peace.

Save the Earth Comic Strips

Brainstorm with the class about our environment. Here are some suggested topics you may wish to discuss:

> pollution
> garbage and other waste
> damaged water supplies
> acid rain
> holes in the ozone
> wasting energy resources
> overpopulation

Ask students to try to create solutions for some of these problems. What are some alternatives to dumping garbage in landfills (which are rapidly filling up) or burning it (which causes air pollution)? What can be done about products that have too much packaging or that use non-biodegradable cartons?

Have the class work together to create a comic strip superhero or heroine who is capable of stopping litterbugs and persuading people to clean up the environment. Design physical features, a costume, a personality, a mission, and a name for the superhero(ine).

Provide students with poster-size oaktag for each comic strip. Let the children use markers or paint to create each strip.

Allow students to extend the comic strip over a few weeks' time if possible so that the superhero(ine)'s character may develop.

Display the comic strips along the wall outside the classroom or in a display case for the whole school to read and enjoy.

Wheel of Knowledge

(for two to three players)

MATERIALS:

4" x 4" oaktag square
pencil
crayons or markers
8" x 8" piece of oaktag
9" x 12" construction paper
tape

DIRECTIONS:

1. To make the spinner, divide the oaktag square into 4 sections, as shown. Number the sections and color each one a different color.
2. Punch a hole through the center of the square with a pencil point. Leave the pencil in the center of the spinner.
3. Think up different topics with which students should be familiar, such as government, cultures, languages, education, technology, history, economy, and ecology. Write out a term used in one of these areas on pieces of construction paper, with one letter of the term written on each piece.
4. Tape the papers in order to the chalkboard with the blank sides facing out. Write the name of the topic above the papers to indicate to students what type of

word it might be.
5. Choose one student to turn the letters. Then have each player spin the spinner to see how many points he or she will receive if the guess is correct. The player then guesses a letter that might be part of the word. If correct, a turner, who knows the answer, flips the paper with that letter on it so it will face the players. Then next player goes.
6. Continue until someone guesses the word on his or her turn. The player who guesses the word correctly gets double the points shown on the spinner. Then play a new round with another term.
7. The player with the most points after the agreed-upon number of rounds is the winner.

Famous Art Charades

Display some books about art in the classroom and encourage students to look through them. Include books with paintings, sculptures, photographs, drawings, and stained glass.

To play a charades-type game, students will need to choose one work of art others might be familiar with and write it on a slip of paper. Place all the papers in a hat.

Make some rules with the class about how to introduce the work of art they will pick from the hat. For example, a painting may be indicated by drawing a large square in the air, and a sculpture may be symbolized by pretending to hammer-and-chisel an imaginary statue.

For a title with more than one word, tell students to indicate this with the corresponding number of fingers. If a particular word is to be acted out, raise that number of fingers before acting. To act out syllables in a word, place the number of syllables (shown by fingers) on the forearm after showing which word it is.

Words may be acted out in a rhyme, or "sounds like ___" manner. For these words, have students sign which word or syllable is being demonstrated, then pull on one ear.

If a student knows the title being acted out is the one he or she contributed, that student should stop guessing and just enjoy the charade.

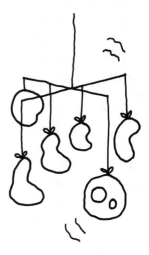

Our Communities

Name _____

Different types of communities exist all over the world. Read the words below. Then write a definition for each community, and tell where this kind of community might be found.

1. barrio _____
_____
_____

2. village _____
_____
_____

3. ghetto _____
_____
_____

4. city _____
_____
_____

5. hamlet _____
_____
_____

6. kibbutz _____
_____
_____

Classroom Kibbutz

Our Classroom Kibbutz!

Gather the class together for a discussion. Discuss what a *kibbutz* is. Explain that a kibbutz is a type of Jewish community in Israel. All the members of each community own the kibbutz together. People must work together to collect food, build homes and schools, educate children, and provide medical care.

Tell students that some members on the kibbutz may work outside the community. The money these people earn is given to the kibbutz. Many members in a kibbutz work within the community for goods and services instead of money. They are given daily jobs by a work committee. Each member of a kibbutz may work on any committee, and may vote on community decisions.

Adults and children live in separate places on a kibbutz. The needs of the community are put before the needs of a family. Children on a kibbutz eat together, sleep in the same quarters, and are schooled together. Mothers and fathers visit their children throughout the day and evening, but live in their own quarters on the kibbutz.

Ask students to imagine what it is like to live on a kibbutz. Help the class come up with a system to form a classroom kibbutz. Have students suggest different committees (i.e., setting up the room each morning, cleaning up the room each afternoon, party coordinator, taking care of class pets, and so on). Let students nominate classmates as heads of the various committees. Then have each committee come up with job descriptions and rules for its members. The rest of the class may vote on each committee's suggestions.

After the committees are in place and the classroom kibbutz has been operating for several weeks, gather the class together for another discussion. Encourage the children to tell what they like and dislike about their kibbutz. Ask students if they have a better understanding of what life on a real kibbutz is like, and why some people enjoy living in such a community. If possible, invite someone who has lived or spent time on a kibbutz to come to the classroom and discuss his or her experiences with the class.

Population Explosion

Name _____

The world population is increasing at a rapid rate. Find out the approximate populations of the countries listed below, and write them in the spaces provided.

1. Australia _____
2. Japan _____
3. Canada _____
4. United States _____
5. South Africa _____
6. Brazil _____
7. China _____
8. Mexico _____
9. France _____
10. Sweden _____
11. Kenya _____
12. Peru _____
13. India _____
14. United Kingdom _____
15. Finland _____

Languages of the World

Name _____

Write the official languages of the countries listed below in the spaces provided.

1. India _____

2. Australia _____

3. Canada _____

4. Kenya _____

5. Peru _____

6. Hong Kong _____

7. Japan _____

8. South Africa _____

9. Mexico _____

10. Denmark _____

11. Italy _____

12. Israel _____

13. China _____

14. Brazil _____

15. Netherlands _____

Of the countries listed, which language is spoken most?

_____

It's Customary

Have a class discussion about different customs and social norms from around the world. Start the discussion off by providing students with some examples of things that are unique to other regions, such as:

> It is considered unacceptable to touch the top of anyone's head—especially a child's—in many parts of Asia.

> Belching after a good meal is considered to be a compliment to the chef for people in Taiwan. However, it is considered rude to eat or drink while walking in public streets.

> Members of traditional Japanese families take hot baths together.

> Children in France celebrate their name days, which are usually saints' feast days, instead of their birthdays.

Ask volunteers to name some customs from other countries that are different from the ones in their own country. Then have students think of customs that are unique to their country. Write each custom on a separate piece of paper. Have students ask their families and friends if they know of any unusual customs, and write these down as well. Then collate all the papers into a customs book, which may be placed in the classroom social studies center for all to enjoy.

Classroom Countries

To encourage a greater understanding of diplomacy between nations, divide the class into groups of approximately five students each. Tell each group that it will represent an imaginary country.

Ask students to choose names for their countries. Then create an 11" x 17" world "map" of these countries. Be sure to include bodies of water, mountains, and other important geographical information.

After the map is completed, write down a list of "facts" about each imaginary country. Some suggested information:

> population
> climate
> natural resources
> type of government
> economy
> education
> religion

For example, you may write: "The country of Zolo has three million inhabitants, who live primarily in two main cities. Zolo has very little agriculture, but is an important manufacturer of automobiles and clothing. The democratic government provides free education to all children from the ages of three to eighteen."

Duplicate the map and fact sheets for each group. Then come up with some situations and problems for the groups to solve by working together. For example, you may tell the members of two countries to solve a border dispute that involves land surrounding an important river. Or you may ask two countries to work out a trade agreement involving manufactured goods and natural resources.

After the groups are familiar with each other, ask each group to help think of situations for other groups. If students seem interested in their imaginary countries, ask them to create travel brochures or mini-history books about their countries.

Class Cultures Display

1. Discuss the creation of a Cultural Awareness Display with the class. Encourage students to think of objects from different cultures that might interest them. Tell the class that objects that sometimes reveal a specific culture include:

> holiday decorations and items (Menorah, kinara, dragon)
> clothing (sari, kimono, dashiki)
> cooking utensils (wok, bamboo steamer)
> foods (curry, enchilada, sushi)
> musical instruments (bagpipes, maracas)
> types of bedding (straw mat, futon)
> types of housing (igloo, high-rise apartment building)

2. Ask students to bring in things from home they would like to show their classmates. Remind students that objects need not be from faraway places; they could be everyday things used right in their own country. Finally, caution the class that the objects will be handled and, if possible, used.

3. Place all these objects on a table. Encourage each student who has brought in an item to share its origin and use with the class. Ask each student to write a short paragraph about his or her item on an index card and place it on the table next to the item.

4. Invite other classes and parents to view the display. Class guides should be ready to answer any questions visitors may have.

Home Sweet Home Bulletin Board

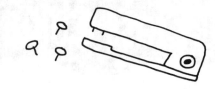

MATERIALS:

map of area where students live
crayons or markers
large sheet of white paper or oaktag
scissors
lined paper
stapler or push pins
different-colored yarn

DIRECTIONS:

1. Study a map of the area in which students live. Observe such things as the shape and size of the area, types of roadways, distances from one end to the other, and the names of roads and familiar landmarks. Research geological differences of the land, and the bodies of water found in the area (rivers, lakes, ponds).

2. Form groups of students who will create local maps of their communities. Maps should include roadways, water areas, mountains, hills, and other surface differences.

3. When the maps are complete, add the names of places in the area: neighborhood names, towns, developments, and other important landmarks.

4. Have students research the organizations, agencies, buildings, government offices, interesting facts and myths, and tourist attractions in the area. The class may also form groups for the topics that interest them the most.

5. Write short essays on the topics stating locations as well.

6. Attach the maps and essays to a bulletin board with the title, "Did You Know..." Attach a strand of different-colored yarn to each essay and tack the other end to the location where the featured place can be found on one of the maps.

Recommended Reading

The following is a list of books that will give students a feel for the stories, games, and songs of countries other than their own. Share some of these books with the class when studying these countries.

1. *The Singing Sack*, compiled by Helen East (A&C Black Publishers, Ltd., 1989)

2. *Step It Down: Games, Plays, Songs, and Stories From the Afro-American Heritage* by Bessie Jones and Bess Lomax Hawes (Univ. of Georgia Press, 1987)

3. *100 Craft Projects From Around the World* by William Reed, Jr. (Olive Press, 1982)

4. *Games of the World* by Frederic Greenfield (UNICEF/Plenary Publishing International, 1975)

5. *Stories to Solve: Folktales From Around the World* by George Shannon (Morrow, 1991)

6. *The Shining Princess and Other Japanese Legends* retold by Eric Quayle (Arcade, 1989)

Fruit Dumplings

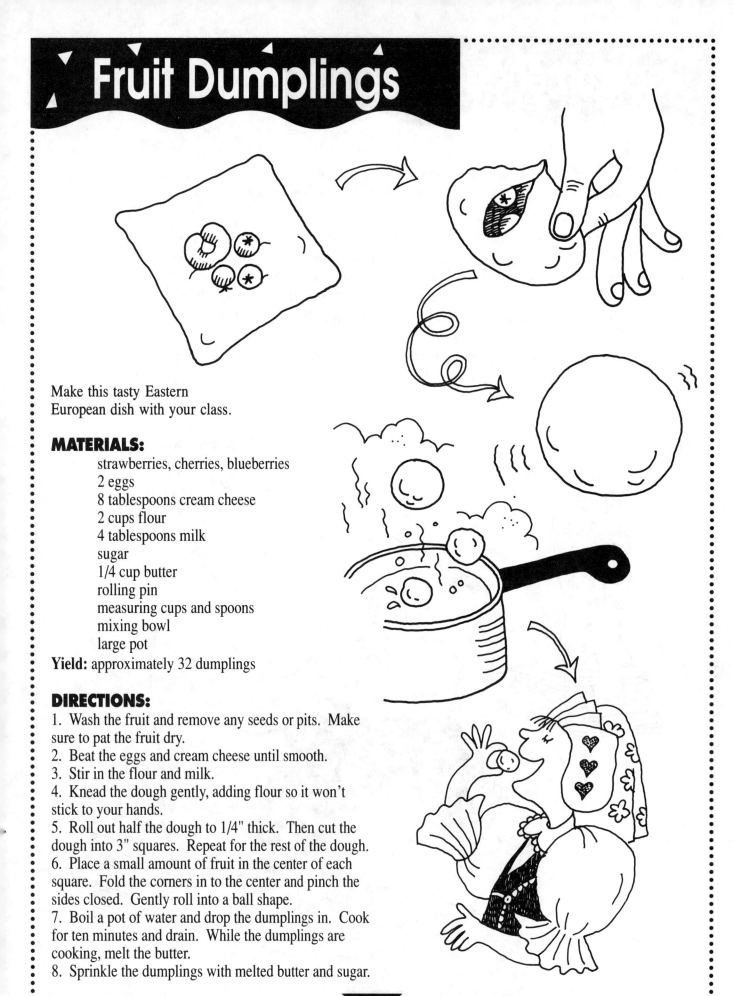

Make this tasty Eastern European dish with your class.

MATERIALS:

strawberries, cherries, blueberries
2 eggs
8 tablespoons cream cheese
2 cups flour
4 tablespoons milk
sugar
1/4 cup butter
rolling pin
measuring cups and spoons
mixing bowl
large pot

Yield: approximately 32 dumplings

DIRECTIONS:

1. Wash the fruit and remove any seeds or pits. Make sure to pat the fruit dry.
2. Beat the eggs and cream cheese until smooth.
3. Stir in the flour and milk.
4. Knead the dough gently, adding flour so it won't stick to your hands.
5. Roll out half the dough to 1/4" thick. Then cut the dough into 3" squares. Repeat for the rest of the dough.
6. Place a small amount of fruit in the center of each square. Fold the corners in to the center and pinch the sides closed. Gently roll into a ball shape.
7. Boil a pot of water and drop the dumplings in. Cook for ten minutes and drain. While the dumplings are cooking, melt the butter.
8. Sprinkle the dumplings with melted butter and sugar.

70

Mask Making

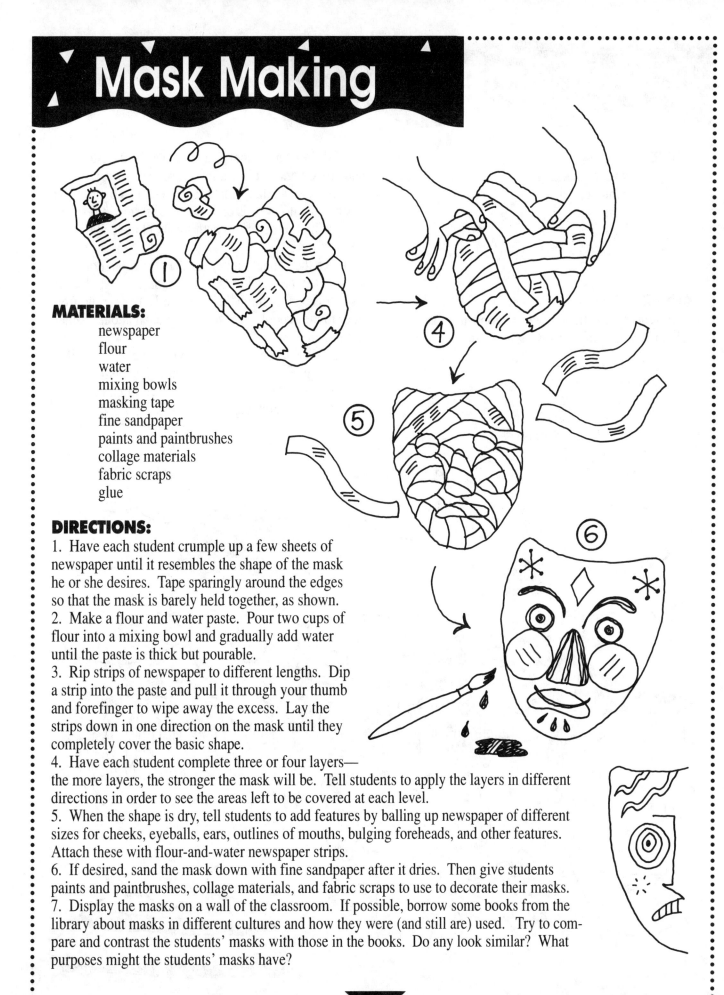

MATERIALS:

- newspaper
- flour
- water
- mixing bowls
- masking tape
- fine sandpaper
- paints and paintbrushes
- collage materials
- fabric scraps
- glue

DIRECTIONS:

1. Have each student crumple up a few sheets of newspaper until it resembles the shape of the mask he or she desires. Tape sparingly around the edges so that the mask is barely held together, as shown.

2. Make a flour and water paste. Pour two cups of flour into a mixing bowl and gradually add water until the paste is thick but pourable.

3. Rip strips of newspaper to different lengths. Dip a strip into the paste and pull it through your thumb and forefinger to wipe away the excess. Lay the strips down in one direction on the mask until they completely cover the basic shape.

4. Have each student complete three or four layers—the more layers, the stronger the mask will be. Tell students to apply the layers in different directions in order to see the areas left to be covered at each level.

5. When the shape is dry, tell students to add features by balling up newspaper of different sizes for cheeks, eyeballs, ears, outlines of mouths, bulging foreheads, and other features. Attach these with flour-and-water newspaper strips.

6. If desired, sand the mask down with fine sandpaper after it dries. Then give students paints and paintbrushes, collage materials, and fabric scraps to use to decorate their masks.

7. Display the masks on a wall of the classroom. If possible, borrow some books from the library about masks in different cultures and how they were (and still are) used. Try to compare and contrast the students' masks with those in the books. Do any look similar? What purposes might the students' masks have?

Welcome Banner

MATERIALS:

crayons or markers
construction paper
scissors
collage materials
glue
tape

DIRECTIONS:

1. Research the different words people use to say "Hello." Some ways of saying hello are:

Jambo—Swahili
Bonjour—French
Shalom—Hebrew
Kon Ni Chi Wa—Japanese
Buenos Dias—Spanish
Guten Tag—German
Ni Hao—Mandarin

2. Make a giant banner featuring the words listed, and any others that you know. Use the paper, writing materials, and collage materials to create a banner that has the "Hello" words on it, as well as drawings or designs that represent something about the countries being featured.

3. Place the banner on or near the classroom door so visitors can be welcomed by it. Another great place to hang this banner might be in the hallway near the front door to the school. Talk to the principal about displaying it there!

4. Begin each school day by saying "Hello" in a different language. Choose a student to decide the language of the day, and encourage the children to research other greetings.

Tostones Recipe

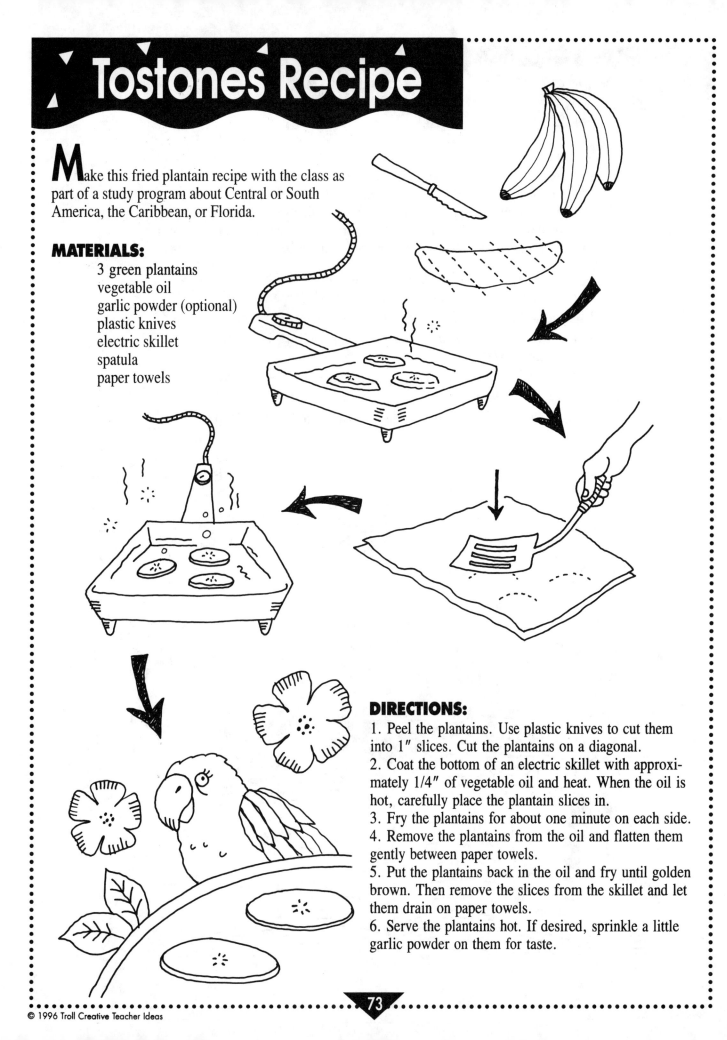

Make this fried plantain recipe with the class as part of a study program about Central or South America, the Caribbean, or Florida.

MATERIALS:

3 green plantains
vegetable oil
garlic powder (optional)
plastic knives
electric skillet
spatula
paper towels

DIRECTIONS:

1. Peel the plantains. Use plastic knives to cut them into 1″ slices. Cut the plantains on a diagonal.
2. Coat the bottom of an electric skillet with approximately 1/4″ of vegetable oil and heat. When the oil is hot, carefully place the plantain slices in.
3. Fry the plantains for about one minute on each side.
4. Remove the plantains from the oil and flatten them gently between paper towels.
5. Put the plantains back in the oil and fry until golden brown. Then remove the slices from the skillet and let them drain on paper towels.
6. Serve the plantains hot. If desired, sprinkle a little garlic powder on them for taste.

Recommended Reading

Locate some or all of the books below about different cultures in your school or local library. Place these books on a bookshelf in the reading or social studies center in your classroom. After students have had a chance to read some of the books, discuss any comments they may make about the similarities and differences between themselves and the characters in the books.

1. *Journey to the Soviet Union* by **Samantha Smith** (Little, Brown, 1985)
2. *The Finding* by Nina Bawden (Lothrop, Lee & Shepard, 1985)
3. *Crutches* by Peter Hartling (Lothrop, Lee & Shepard, 1988)
4. *The Sea Wedding and Other Stories From Estonia* by Peggy Hoffman (Dillon Press, 1978)
5. *Twelve Iron Sandals: And Other Czechoslovak Tales* by Vit Horejs (Prentice Hall, 1985)
6. *The Bomber's Moon* by Betty Vander Els (Farrar, Straus & Giroux, 1985)

Favorite Things Guide

Tell students that many people all over the world have a favorite thing to do, whether it is a job, a hobby, a sport, or another interesting thing. Go around the room and ask each student what he or she enjoys doing most.

Write students' comments on the chalkboard. Then have them help graph the responses to see what the most popular choices are.

After students' choices have been discussed, ask each child to write up a step-by-step guide for doing his or her favorite thing. Tell students to make sure the sequence is in proper order. Encourage students to give their guides to friends to read to see if the instructions are clear.

Ask students to provide illustrations or photographs with the guide to better explain any complicated parts.

When the guides are completed, have each student give a short oral presentation, using his or her guide for reference and illustration. Encourage students to ask questions or critique the guide. Does it make the topic sound interesting? Is it clear and understandable?

After all the children have made their presentations, place the guides on a table in the reading center for all to see.

Celebrations Word Search

Name _____

Find the names of the holidays listed below in the word search, then circle them. The words may be written up, down, forward, backward, or diagonally.

```
M A A Z N A W K C H R I S
H A W N Z A A D O I M I N
T I Y C R V A L R E N S D
N N K D S M H C R T I K L
A D S M A R D I G R A S P
S E W A S Y L T P I N A F
A P D O M I N I O N D A Y
B E G R E T S A E S T A M
I N A W I N S K B A S A N
X D O N L A V I N R A C O
M E K E U P Y O R M I N N
U N I T E F O R P H J V H
Y C F E A S K E R C C D O
N E W Y E A R S E V E M E
O D M I S K O I P J U I C
Y A D S N E R D L I H C E
B Y A D G N I X O B T K H
```

Kwanzaa	Christmas	Basanth	New Year's Eve
May Day	Easter	Boxing Day	Independence Day
Mardi Gras	Carnival	Dominion Day	Children's Day

What Should I Do?

Children all over the world go through very similar experiences and development. Encourage students to write a letter stating something that might be confusing, interesting, and/or incomprehensible to them. They do not need to sign their names.

Form a circle and read one letter aloud to the class. (Caution the class that this is not a chance to make fun of a classmate but rather to help someone. Try to choose letters that will not cause too much controversy or embarrassment.)

Ask students for ideas to solve the problem in each letter, or for comments and opinions on what has been stated in each letter. Students may add their own experiences if they are similar to ones described in the letters, and tell what the outcome was for them.

Designate a drop-off spot for more letters if the question-and-answer sessions are successful. This spot might be a box on the teacher's desk, or a file box in the writing center.

HAVE A PROBLEM?

Foreign Foods

Name _____

A lot of foods we eat and know originated in other countries. Read the list of foods below. Then identify the country or culture where each was developed on the lines provided.

1. quiche _____

2. roast beef and
   Yorkshire pudding _____

3. herring _____

4. sauerkraut _____

5. couscous _____

6. gyro _____

7. sushi _____

8. tortilla _____

9. curry _____

10. pasta _____

11. chocolate _____

12. matzoh _____

13. pita bread _____

14. shortbread _____

15. caviar _____

16. croissant _____

17. scone _____

18. tea _____

Can you think of other foods that originated elsewhere? Write the foods and their places of origin on the lines below. _____

_____

_____

Sarah, Plain and Tall

Read or assign the book *Sarah, Plain and Tall* by Patricia MacLachlan (HarperCollins, 1985) to the class during a study unit about post-Civil War America. Have a class discussion about the book, and ask such reading comprehension questions as:

How do you think Sarah felt when she arrived at the cabin?

Why do you think she decided to stay?

How would you feel about having a "mail-order" mother?

Do you think Jacob did the right thing by placing an advertisement for a wife?

Sarah described herself as "plain and tall." How would you describe her?

Why were each of the characters in this book lonely?

Use extension activities as ways to reinforce the story's message. Some suggestions are:

Pretend you are a father or mother living alone with your children in the 1800s. Write an advertisement for a mail-order spouse. What kinds of qualities would you look for in a person?

Rewrite a chapter or scene from the book from Jacob's, Caleb's, or Sarah's point of view.

Pretend that you have left your home, as Sarah did, to live a new life elsewhere. Where would you like to go? What things would you miss about your old life? Write a letter to your family from your new home.

What is your favorite part of the book? Draw a picture that shows this scene.

79

Number the Stars

The book *Number the Stars* by Lois Lowry (Dell, 1990) details the efforts of the Danish Resistance during World War II. Annemarie, a ten-year-old girl, learns about bravery as she watches common people risk their lives to smuggle their Jewish comrades across the sea to Sweden where they will be safe from the Nazis.

Read or assign this book during a study unit on World War II, or while discussing religious persecution throughout history. Ask discussion questions, such as:

> What were some of the changes that took place in Denmark after the Nazis arrived?
>
> How would you feel if you were Annemarie and had to hide your friend?
>
> How did Annemarie's mother keep the Nazi soldier from looking in the casket?
>
> Why did Annemarie have to deliver the packet to Uncle Henrik?
>
> What was special about the handkerchief?
>
> Why was Peter killed?
>
> How do you think Annemarie felt at the end of the story?

As an extension activity, have students write newspaper accounts about Nazi-occupied Denmark during World War II. Encourage children to include as many details as they can in their stories. Or, have students role play as pen pals, with some students portraying Ellen or Annemarie, and other students asking them questions about the war.

Nettie's Trip

Name _____

Read the book *Nettie's Trip South* by Ann Turner (Macmillan, 1987). This story is about a ten-year-old girl who visits the South during the 1800s, and how she reacts to slavery.

Pretend that you are a visitor to the South during the days of slavery. Write a letter home that tells about what you have observed and experienced. Be sure to use as much detail as you can to describe your trip.

_____ ,

_____

_____

_____

_____

_____

_____

_____

_____

_____

_____

_____

International T-Shirt Day

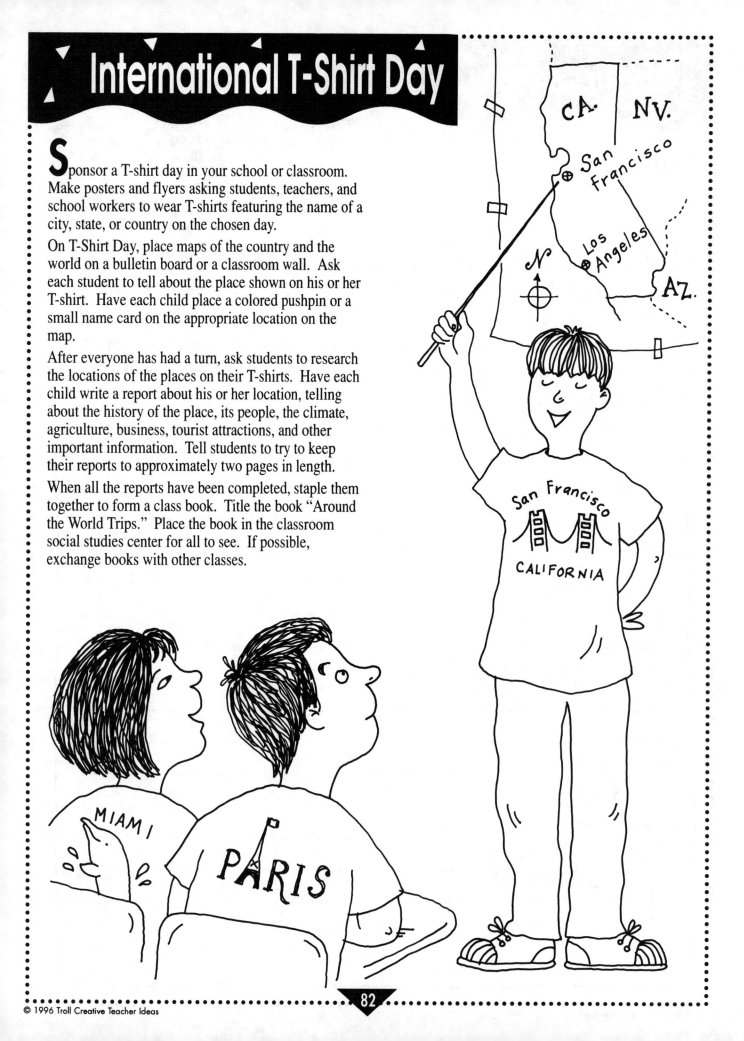

Sponsor a T-shirt day in your school or classroom. Make posters and flyers asking students, teachers, and school workers to wear T-shirts featuring the name of a city, state, or country on the chosen day.

On T-Shirt Day, place maps of the country and the world on a bulletin board or a classroom wall. Ask each student to tell about the place shown on his or her T-shirt. Have each child place a colored pushpin or a small name card on the appropriate location on the map.

After everyone has had a turn, ask students to research the locations of the places on their T-shirts. Have each child write a report about his or her location, telling about the history of the place, its people, the climate, agriculture, business, tourist attractions, and other important information. Tell students to try to keep their reports to approximately two pages in length.

When all the reports have been completed, staple them together to form a class book. Title the book "Around the World Trips." Place the book in the classroom social studies center for all to see. If possible, exchange books with other classes.

Autograph Mania

Ask each student to choose a famous person from history to represent for this game. Tell students to keep their identities secret from everyone except the teacher. Then have students write short reports about their chosen person.

From students' reports, make a list of 3 clues for each of the famous names chosen. Reproduce the list once for each child in the class and distribute.

When the game begins, all students must try to guess each historical figure's name based on the clues they were given. When a student correctly guesses a famous person's identity, he or she may then get the autograph.

The player who collects all the autographs first wins.

When the game is over, place all the reports in the social studies center for all to read.

Make the Connection

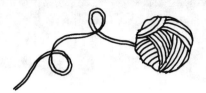

MATERIALS:

markers
18″ × 24″ pieces of oaktag
hole puncher
30″ lengths of yarn (10 different colors)

DIRECTIONS:

1. Write the names of ten well-known U.S. Presidents on an 18″ × 24″ piece of oaktag. Then write in random order a list of things for which these presidents are known on another piece. Some suggested matchings:

George Washington—made Commander-in-Chief of colonial army in 1775, first President of the United States

Thomas Jefferson—wrote the Declaration of Independence, events during his administration include the Louisiana Purchase and the Lewis and Clark Expedition

Franklin D. Roosevelt—elected to four terms, New Deal began during his administration

John F. Kennedy—established U.S. Peace Corps, astronaut and satellite orbiting greatly developed

Bill Clinton—advocated health care benefits for all Americans

2. Punch a hole next to each name and accomplishment. Make the holes about 1″ to the right of the presidents' names and 1″ to the left of their accomplishments, as shown.

3. Attach the different colored 30″ lengths of yarn to the holes next to the presidents' names.

4. To play, place the oaktag pieces on easels. Then have students match the name to the accomplishment by threading the free end of each yarn length into a hole (next to the correct match) on the other piece of oaktag.

5. Create different versions of the game, such as:

famous explorers
world leaders
Revolutionary War figures
Civil War figures
women's history
African American history
civil rights leaders
scientists and inventors

What's Her Name?

Name _____

Fill in the names (may be last names only) of the famous women described in the clues.

Across

1. Refused to give up her seat on a bus to a white man.
5. Colonial patriot who made the first American flag.
6. Served as an interpreter for Lewis and Clark.
8. Indian nun who won the Nobel Peace Prize in 1979.
10. Prime minister of India who was assassinated while in office.
13. American abolitionist.
14. Founder of the American Red Cross.

Down

2. Fought for human rights while married to a U.S. President.
3. Overcame blindness and deafness to become a famous author and lecturer.
4. First woman doctor in the U.S.
7. Led French armies against the English in the Hundred Years' War.
8. Anthropologist and author.
9. Helped hundreds of slaves escape on the Underground Railroad.
11. Campaigned for women's rights in the late 1800s.
12. Author of *Little Women*.

Native American Heroes

Name _____

Write a brief description for each of the Native Americans below, telling what their accomplishments were and from what tribal nations they descended.

1. Jim Thorpe _____

_____

_____

_____

2. Pocahontas _____

_____

_____

_____

3. Chief Joseph _____

_____

_____

_____

4. Henry Chee Dodge _____

_____

_____

_____

5. Susan La Flesche _____

_____

_____

_____

Presidential Professions

Name _____

What kinds of jobs have people had before they became Presidents of the United States? Most U. S. presidents began their careers as lawyers. Some presidents, however, have had different—and unusual—jobs.

Unscramble the career for each president below. On a separate piece of paper, write a short essay about one of the presidents, focusing on his life before he became president.

1. George Washington   YRROEVUS _____

2. Thomas Jefferson   TCHCRAETI _____

3. Andrew Johnson   RLOAIT _____

4. Theodore Roosevelt   RNARCHE _____

5. Woodrow Wilson   HAETRCE _____

6. Herbert Hoover   NGEEERNI _____

7. Harry S Truman   SNISSNBAMUE _____

8. Dwight D. Eisenhower   RALEGNE _____

9. James E. Carter   RRMEAF _____

10. Ronald Reagan   RTCAO _____

Who Said It?

Name _____

Identify the speaker of each quotation below. Use the names in the box at the bottom of the page to help you. Be careful—extra names have been added to trick you!

1. Ask not what your country can do for you; ask what you can do for your country.

_____

2. Never in the field of human conflict was so much owed by so many to so few.

_____

3. I came, I saw, I conquered. _____

4. That's one small step for a man, one giant leap for mankind. _____

5. A house divided against itself cannot stand. _____

6. I shall return. _____

7. Early to bed and early to rise, makes a man healthy, wealthy, and wise.

_____

8. Speak softly and carry a big stick. _____

9. The only thing we have to fear is fear itself. _____

10. I only regret that I have but one life to lose for my country. _____

11. The buck stops here. _____

12. Genius is one percent inspiration and 99 percent perspiration.

_____

Christopher Columbus	**Benjamin Franklin**	**Nathan Hale**
Thomas Edison	**Frederick Douglass**	**General Douglas MacArthur**
Martin Luther King, Jr.	**John F. Kennedy**	**Napoleon**
Julius Caesar	**Abraham Lincoln**	**Franklin D. Roosevelt**
Harry S Truman	**Theodore Roosevelt**	**Winston Churchill**
Neil Armstrong	**Albert Einstein**	**Patrick Henry**

Medical Breakthroughs

Name _____

Each of the scientists below made significant contributions to the world of medicine. On the lines provided, write a short description of a medical breakthrough made by each person.

1. Louis Pasteur _____
   _____

2. Gregor Mendel _____
   _____

3. Edward Jenner _____
   _____

4. Jonas Salk _____
   _____

5. Charles Gerhardt _____
   _____

6. René Laënnec _____
   _____

7. Crawford W. Long and W.T.G. Morton _____
   _____

8. Joseph Lister _____
   _____

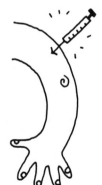

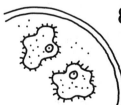

Can you think of other people who have made medical discoveries that have changed the world? Write about them on a separate piece of paper.

Famous African Americans

Name _____

Circle the *last* names of the famous African Americans hidden in the word search puzzle below. The words may be hidden forward, backward, up, down, or diagonally.

```
T W H E A T L E Y E V R A G
D Y U L H R E K L A W K V Y
R E V R A C H I S O L M Y E
E L U G R W N B D L S O O L
W L N K I O A U A U S R U A
S I A L Y K B H B W A R N H
K N M V E O S I V Y L I G U
R G B R I R G W N L G S E G
A T U S A A R O N S U O H H
P O T M A Y S L K I O N S E
S N E W O N O S R E D N A S
```

Hank Aaron	Marian Anderson	Arthur Ashe
Josephine Baker	Ralph Bunche	George Washington Carver
Frederick Douglass	Dr. Charles Richard Drew	W.E.B. Du Bois
Duke Ellington	Marcus Garvey	Alex Haley
Langston Hughes	Dr. Martin Luther King, Jr.	Thurgood Marshall
Willie Mays	Toni Morrison	Jesse Owens
Rosa Parks	Jackie Robinson	Harriet Tubman
Alice Walker	Phillis Wheatley	Andrew Jackson Young, Jr.

After you have completed the puzzle, write a short biography about one of the people listed in the box above. Tell about the person's childhood and education, and how he or she became famous.

Money of the World

Name _____

Fill in the missing letters to show the term for the basic unit of money in each of these countries.

1. Italy   __ i r a

2. China   y __ a n

3. Canada   __ o l __ a r

4. Poland   z __ o t __

5. South Korea   w __ n

6. Pakistan   r __ p e __

7. Argentina   __ u s __ r a l

8. Japan   __ e __

9. Egypt   p __ __ n d

10. Greece   __ r a __ h m __

Answers

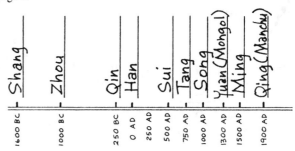

page 9

1. Hanging Gardens of Babylon—Were probably built by King Nebuchadnezzar II between 605 and 562 B.C. It is believed that slaves watered the gardens by turning screws to lift water from the Euphrates River.

2. Temple of Artemis at Ephesus—Was built about 550 B.C. The building was made entirely of marble except for the roof, which was covered with tiles. The temple burned down in 356 B.C.

3. Egyptian Pyramids at Giza—The oldest and best-preserved of the Seven Wonders. These pyramids were built as tombs for the Egyptian kings about 2600-2500 B.C.

4. Colossus of Rhodes—A huge bronze statue built to honor the Greek god, Helios. The statue was about 120 feet high and took twelve years for the Greek sculptor Chares to complete.

5. Lighthouse of Alexandria—Was over 400 feet high and was completed in the 200s B.C. The lighthouse stood on the island of Pharos, and the word *pharos* eventually came to mean *lighthouse*.

6. Statue of Zeus at Olympia—May have been the most famous statue of the ancient world. It was made about 435 B.C. and dedicated to Zeus, the king of all the Greek gods.

7. Mausoleum at Halicarnassus—Was built around 353 B.C. as a tomb for Mausolus, a ruler in the Persian Empire. The tomb became so famous that all large tombs today are called mausoleums.

Answers for modern-day wonders will vary. Possible answers include the Taj Mahal; World Trade Center; Mount Rushmore; Great Wall of China; Eiffel Tower; Leaning Tower of Pisa; Palace at Versailles; Space Needle in Seattle.

page 10

1. 1812-1815	6. 1608
2. 1673	7. 1898
3. 1967	8. 1920
4. 1784	9. 1642
5. 1867	10. 1774

page 11

1. Southeast	6. Southeast
2. Northeast	7. Plains
3. Southwest	8. Arctic region
4. Southwest	9. California
5. Far North	10. Plains

page 12

1. D	6. I
2. F	7. C
3. H	8. E
4. J	9. A
5. B	10. G

page 15

1. 1804	6. 1620
2. 44 A.D.	7. 1885
3. 1787	8. 3500 B.C.
4. 1903	9. 1839
5. 1873	10. 1783

page 16

Events that did not happen in the 20th century:
Columbus sets sail for a new route to India.
The automobile is invented.
Magellan circumnavigates the globe.
Ellis Island opens the door for immigration to America.
Thousands of people move to California to cash in on the gold rush.

page 17

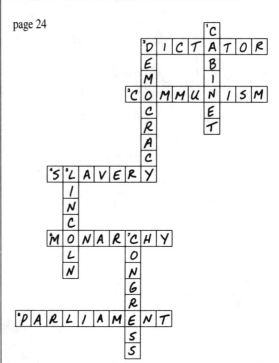

page 18

1. Leningrad	5. Battle of Hastings	8. Battle of Midway
2. Waterloo	6. Trojan War	9. The Alamo
3. Battle of Saratoga	7. Pearl Harbor	10. Battle of New Orleans
4. Gettysburg		

page 23

1. Victorian 2. Greenland 3. Roman 4. economy 5. Thomas Edison 6. Inuit 7. Sahara 8. Pacific 9. Franklin 10. Pasteur

page 24

Answers

page 25

Europe: France, Denmark, Poland
North America: United States of America, Canada, Mexico
South America: Brazil, Peru, Argentina
Asia: Japan, China, Thailand, Israel, India
Africa: Kenya, South Africa

page 26

1. 40° east longitude, 10° north latitude
2. 40° east longitude, 0° south latitude
3. the Sahara Desert
4. 10° east longitude
5. Zaïre

page 29

page 36

Answers will vary.

pages 38-39

Weather Chart
1. Michigan or Hawaii
2. Hawaii
3. Hawaii
4. Nevada

Summer Olympics
1. Cuba
2. Bulgaria
3. Bulgaria
4. Unified Team
5. Denmark

Air Distances
1. Montreal to Berlin; Beijing to Rio de Janeiro; London to Rio de Janeiro
2. Warsaw to Berlin
   London to Berlin
   Montreal to Berlin
   Beijing to Berlin
   Montreal to Rio de Janeiro
   Beijing to Melbourne
   London to Rio de Janeiro
   Warsaw to Rio de Janeiro
   Warsaw to Melbourne
   Montreal to Melbourne
   London to Melbourne
   Beijing to Rio de Janeiro
3. Montreal to Rio de Janeiro
4. Montreal to Berlin; Warsaw to Berlin; London to Melbourne; Warsaw to Melbourne; Beijing to Rio de Janeiro; London to Rio de Janeiro; Montreal to Rio de Janeiro

pages 40-41

Answers will vary.

page 42

1. Take Genessee Street East to 690 East to 81 North. From 81 North, make a right onto Airport Blvd.
2. Approximately 5 miles.
3. Take 81 South to South Avenue and make a right onto South Avenue.
4. South.
5. South Avenue and Velasko Road.

page 43

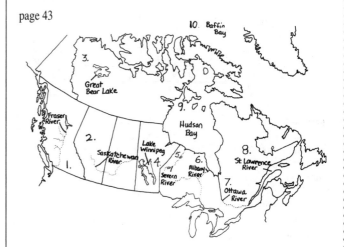

Answers

page 44

Mississippi River—Minnesota, Mississippi, Wisconsin, Iowa, Illinois, Missouri, Kentucky, Tennessee, Arkansas, Louisiana

Missouri River—Montana, North Dakota, South Dakota, Missouri, Nebraska, Iowa, Kansas

Snake River—Wyoming, Idaho, Washington, Oregon

Hudson River—New York

Colorado River—Colorado, Utah, Arizona, Nevada, California

Rio Grande—Colorado, New Mexico, Texas

Allegheny River—Pennsylvania, New York

Sacramento River—California

Arkansas River—Colorado, Kansas, Oklahoma, Arkansas

Ohio River—Pennsylvania, Ohio, Indiana, Illinois, West Virginia, Kentucky

page 45

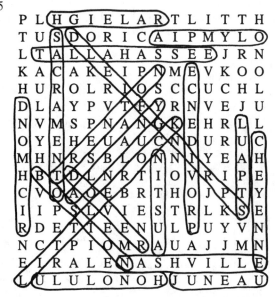

Alaska—Juneau
Arkansas—Little Rock
California—Sacramento
Delaware—Dover
Florida—Tallahassee
Hawaii—Honolulu
Illinois—Springfield
Massachusetts—Boston
Minnesota—St. Paul

New Jersey—Trenton
New York—Albany
North Carolina—Raleigh
Rhode Island—Providence
Tennessee—Nashville
Texas—Austin
Virginia—Richmond
Washington—Olympia
Wyoming—Cheyenne

page 46

Argentina S
India N
Switzerland N
New Zealand S
Canada N
China N
Peru S
Mozambique S

South Korea N
Uruguay S
Finland N
Australia S
Poland N
Mexico N
Egypt N

page 47

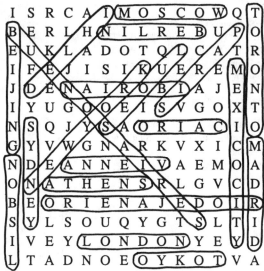

1; 4; 9; 12; 11; 6; 16; 2; 3; 17; 13; 18; 19; 8; 20; 10; 15; 5; 14; 7

page 49

Answers will vary. Possible answers:
1. Great Wall (China)
2. Eiffel Tower (France)
3. Colosseum (Italy)
4. Washington Monument (United States)
5. jungle animals (Kenya)
6. Amazon River (Peru or Brazil)
7. Pyramids of Giza (Egypt)
8. Parthenon (Greece)
9. Machu Picchu (Peru)
10. Red Square (Russia)

page 50

1. Grand Canyon
2. Niagara Falls
3. Mount Everest
4. Dead Sea

5. Sahara Desert
6. Mont Blanc
7. Amazon River
8. Everglades

page 51

1. Magellan—Circumnavigate the globe: Sail west from Spain to Cape Horn/Philippines
2. Cook—Tahiti/New Zealand/Australia/Hawaiian Islands
3. Columbus—West Indies
4. Lewis & Clark—Rocky Mountains/Pacific coast
5. Ericson—Newfoundland
6. Balboa—Isthmus of Panama/Pacific Ocean
7. de Léon—Florida
8. Amundsen—South Pole
9. Polo—China
10. Cortes—Mexico
11. Hudson—Sail north on a river in New York/Bay in Canada
12. Hillary & Norgay—Mount Everest

page 54

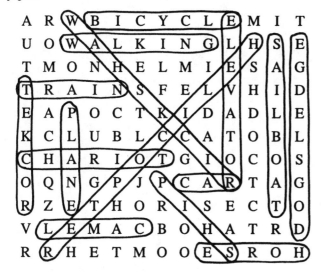

page 61

Answers will vary. Possible answers:

1. barrio—a neighborhood in which most of the people speak Spanish. May be found in large U.S. cities, Spanish-speaking countries or the Philippines.
2. village—a small group of people and buildings. A village is usually smaller than a town. Found in rural areas.
3. ghetto—a slum area often occupied by people of one particular minority group. Found in cities.
4. city—densely populated center for business and the arts. Cities are found within states, counties, or countries around the world.
5. hamlet—a group of people and buildings that is smaller than a village. Found in rural areas.
6. kibbutz—a community in which all the people work together to provide themselves with food, clothing, education, and shelter. Found in Israel.

page 63
Answers may vary.

1. 16.8 million
2. 124 million
3. 26.8 million
4. 248.7 million
5. 40.6 million
6. 148 million
7. 1.151 billion
8. 90 million
9. 56.6 million
10. 8.6 million
11. 25.2 million
12. 22.3 million
13. 866 million
14. 55.5 million
15. 5 million

page 64

1. Hindi
2. English
3. English and French
4. English
5. Spanish and Quechua
6. English and Chinese
7. Japanese
8. Afrikaans, English
9. Spanish
10. Danish
11. Italian
12. Hebrew and Arabic
13. Mandarin (northern Chinese)
14. Portuguese
15. Dutch

Of the countries listed, English is spoken most.

page 76

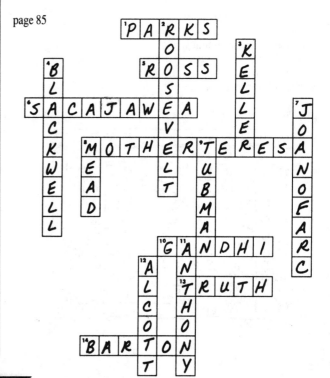

page 78
1. France
2. England
3. Scandinavia
4. Germany
5. North Africa
6. Greece
7. Japan
8. Mexico
9. India
10. Italy
11. Aztecs
12. Israel
13. Middle East
14. Scotland
15. Russia
16. France
17. Scotland
18. China

page 85

Answers

page 86

1. First president of the American Professional Football Association (now known as the National Football League). Sac and Fox.
2. Saved the Jamestown settlers from starving to death; believed to have saved the life of Captain John Smith. Powhatan.
3. Led his people in a war against the U.S. army. Nez Percé.
4. First chairman of the Navajo Tribal Council. Navajo.
5. First female Native American doctor (1889). Omaha/Osage.

page 87

1. surveyor
2. architect
3. tailor
4. rancher
5. teacher
6. engineer
7. businessman
8. general
9. farmer
10. actor

page 88

1. John F. Kennedy
2. Winston Churchill
3. Julius Caesar
4. Neil Armstrong
5. Abraham Lincoln
6. General Douglas MacArthur
7. Benjamin Franklin
8. Théodore Roosevelt
9. Franklin D. Roosevelt
10. Nathan Hale
11. Harry S. Truman
12. Thomas Edison

page 89

1. Louis Pasteur - germ theory; pasteurization
2. Gregor Mendel - genetics
3. Edward Jenner - smallpox vaccine
4. Jonas Salk - polio vaccine
5. Charles Gerhardt - aspirin
6. René Laënnec - stethoscope
7. Crawford W. Long and W.T.G. Morton - ether
8. Joseph Lister - antiseptics

page 90

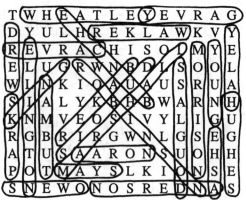

page 91

1. lira
2. yuan
3. dollar
4. zloty
5. won
6. rupee
7. austral
8. yen
9. pound
10. drachma